T0300678

IN THE FOREST
OF METROPOLES

THE GERMAN LIST

Karl-Markus Gauß

IN THE FOREST
OF METROPOLES

TRANSLATED BY
TESS LEWIS

LONDON NEW YORK CALCUTTA

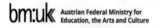

This publication was supported by a grant from the Austrian
Federal Ministry for Education, Arts and Culture,
and the Goethe-Institut India.

NATIONAL ENDOWMENT for the ARTS
arts.gov

This project was supported in part by an award
from the National Endowment for the Arts.

Seagull Books, 2025

Originally published in German as *Im Wald Der Metropolen*
by Karl-Markus Gauß

© Paul Zsolnay Verlag, Vienna, 2010

First published in English translation by Seagull Books, 2025
English translation © Tess Lewis, 2025

ISBN   978 1 8030 9 397 0

British Library Cataloguing-in-Publication Data
A catalogue record for this book is available from the British Library.

Typeset by Seagull Books, Calcutta, India
Printed and bound by WordsWorth India, New Delhi, India

CONTENTS

CHAPTER ONE

The Grimacer of Beaune

It was in Beaune that I saw the wildest grimacer of my life. We'd been warned the place was overrun with tourists by a tourist who was convinced we shared his self-delusion and who believed we were modern nomads simply because we were charting our own course instead of following some travel agency's package deal. The tourist's hatred of other tourists is like that of the provincial for his ilk; this antipathy produces curious self-images, of which the credit-card carrying adventurer is one of the most striking. You meet these types everywhere: they form venturesome crowds in the desert and on high mountain ranges and fleets of them descend on remote islands in the Pacific known exclusively to them. We hadn't planned on spending the night in Beaune, swarming as it is with tourists. But once we'd visited the famous Hôtel-Dieu, we set off in search of lodgings in this sizable small city.

What the Burgundian chancellor Nicolas Rolin and his wife Guigone de Salins intended when they had the Hôtel-Dieu built in 1443 was, in the chancellor's own words, nothing less than the eternal salvation of their souls through this charitable work. For more than 600 years, the Hôtel-Dieu, built on a more generous scale than any previously known, served as a hospital for the poor, offering them religious as well as medical succour. Its Gothic sick ward is 50-metre long and 14-metre wide, and the side walls are lined with beds from which the patients could see the chapel and altar at the front of the Great Hall, allowing them to attend holy mass without having to leave the ward.

A magnificent vaulted roof of ogival arches spans the hall. This elegant ceiling's most interesting feature are the wooden crossbeams that appear to project from the throats of spewing dragons and are decorated with droll faces mounted across from grotesque animal heads. The faces were modelled on prominent citizens of Beaune, and the animal heads—each associated with a particular inhabitant's foolishly grinning face and meant to communicate something of his or her particular character—capture their profligacy for all time. We admired the ingenious functionality with which the ward was equipped for medical purpose and marvelled at the spiritual power it commanded, oriented as it was towards the altar, but most of all we delighted in the presence of the absurdity manifest in the wood construction of the vault that sheltered the ill in a building dedicated to the solemn two-fold goal of healing the body and redeeming the soul. This absurdity was nothing less than a double dose of mockery for the prosperous citizens of Beaune who had contributed to the building and to support of the hospice, in both the ridiculous depiction of their laughing faces and in the animal heads that exposed their avarice, cupidity, obtuseness and immorality.

It was under this vault that I saw him for the first time. He had not turned his eyes upwards; he had no idea there might be anything to see there, perhaps even his own face. He was simply one of the herd, since all tourists are shepherded through the Hôtel-Dieu. He followed the others, and I followed him out of the ward and into the *cour d'honneur,* which offers the best view of the extensive wings, the colourful rooftiles, the dormer windows decorated with wood carvings, the slate-tiles and, off to one side, a well decorated with filigreed ironwork. I followed him as he followed the others from the courtyard into the smaller Salle Saint Hugues, where patients and the elderly who required extended care were housed, and from there into the Salle Saint Nicolas, where the terminally ill and the dying faced their end. We were together in the pharmacy, the kitchens and the rooms with displays of household devices and tools of eras long-past.

He was about my age, wiry, with angular features, close-cropped hair and a curious goatee that extended in a thin, white line from his lower lip to his chin like a painful nick. He seemed alert and, extending his arm to point out some feature of the facade to the woman standing next to him, soon made a painful grimace, further frightening a few children already alarmed at the sight of eighteenth-century amputation shears. He then joined a group of men who had lit their cigarettes in the courtyard.

That evening I saw him again. We were ambling through town after our visit to the Hôtel-Dieu, having exited the circle drawn around the town centre by the old, almost perfectly preserved city walls. The rectangular Place Madeleine is lined with plane trees and there we had found the Auberge Bourguignonne, which contained a small hotel and a restaurant within the dry set masonry of its walls built with thousands upon thousands of pale stones. The dining room was almost completely full when we entered it a few minutes after eight. As is customary in France, the tables were placed very close together with the narrow gaps between them marking a symbolic border. Diners here do not greet those seated at neighbouring tables nor do they listen in on conversations being held less than half a metre away and they most certainly do not encroach on their neighbours' territory by joining in, just as these neighbours also take pains not to overhear others, imperturbably minding their own business, no matter what is going on at the next table. Despite general observance of this cultural convention, French restaurants and bistros, packed tight with tables, still provide no intimate spaces.

The man with the sharply drawn line of a beard was the only single diner in the restaurant. This struck me before we had even taken our seats and I viscerally understood what this meant before I could picture any of the horrifying possibilities. He was seated diagonally to my left, about 4 metres away. When I glanced past my wife's right shoulder, I looked straight into his face, which was in constant motion and displayed a panoply of emotions that were difficult to interpret. As we began our appetizers, he was already busy with his entrée and yet he was more concerned with finding someone who could free him from the constraint of eating alone. This solo diner was completely unaware of the symbolic borders that were meant to be observed in a restaurant like this. He felt free to consider spatial proximity as an invitation to camaraderie. First, he tried with the couple sitting to his left, clearly local residents, who showed little inclination to be taught new customs by the stranger. They responded brusquely to his attempts to draw them into conversation about the dishes that had just been served. They gave a laconic reply and ended the exchange, refusing to be irritated by the man at the neighbouring table or to pay him the slightest attention. The man, it gradually became clear, was from Holland. His French sounded passable, his German, in which he addressed the tourists to his right, no less so. The two Germans, an elegant woman of perhaps fifty and a tall man inclined to stoutness who appeared some eight to ten years younger, let themselves be lured into an exchange of opinions regarding the cuisine and hotel industry in France but then became monosyllabic, not only in conversing with their neighbour but also with each other, no longer confident that their conversation was, in fact, theirs alone. They left the restaurant before all the other guests, as befits two fugitives, without saying goodbye to the man who had been all too eager to be their companion that evening.

Now he sits alone, trying to find something to occupy him, checking the wine bottle yet again, fraternizing with the waiter, looking around the room for help, avidly seeking anyone willing to meet his eye, someone who won't look away, but he finds no one. He remains in the restaurant's public space with only his own company, left to his own devices, and no matter how often this may have happened to him in the past, he still seems unable to get used to it. When he is served dessert, he speaks to himself in the room's dense emptiness, he stretches fitfully, first to one side, then the other before bending forward over the table and jerking backward so abruptly the back of his chair gives a loud creak.

Then his face undergoes a tremendous alteration. Up until now his face had been in constant motion, his expression changing every few seconds. With enormous effort, he strains every muscle in his face, which freezes in an appalling grimace. He presses his square chin against his chest so that the ridges on the nape of his neck protrude. His mouth is clamped shut, his lips pressed together as if in a spasm. From his upper lip a deeply etched wrinkle descends on either side of his mouth to his chin, which seems to swell and is riven by the white line of his goatee. His nasolabial folds extend from the sides of his nose like two long arched incisions to his mouth, where they merge with the folds descending to his chin. He wrinkles his nose so energetically that its root, together with his painfully compressed eyelids, form a single bulge from which emerge innumerable tiny crowfoot pleats.

I am witnessing a psychological natural catastrophe, a monumental spectacle of tormented nature. The room has fallen completely silent—no clatter of dishes or silverware, no laughter or clinking glasses—and in this silence I believe I can hear the man's muscles cramping and contracting, his teeth grinding and his wheezing with the effort this oblivious self-exhibition demands.

Never before have I seen such a dramatic play of facial expressions, not in my childhood, when we staged our world grimacing championships on rainy vacation days and all the neighbourhood children struggled to outdo each other making faces. The solo diner's entire face seems at once swollen and compressed, deformed by some immense force. The expression of his frozen grimace is ambiguous. It is an expression of some unnamed despair but also of a self-contained arrogance and even though finally, after such fretfulness, he sits as immobile as if he were cast in stone, not a single twitch animating his stony face, it seems to me that his countenance still changes every few seconds. I have the impression that now he's grinning, now weeping; now I believe I see the very picture of malevolence, now of pure suffering.

Why are you making such terrible faces? My wife asks me. Because she is familiar with my unprincipled propensity to imitation, she can tell, when she hears me talking on the telephone, who is on the other end of the line, whose tone of voice, speech pattern and dialect I have unintentionally assumed. Although I've never before witnessed anyone abandon himself so completely to a grimace, I was nonetheless sure I had seen this grimace before. But that evening I came no closer to an explanation than on subsequent days.

Messerschmidt: A Note

The entire complex, which includes a magnificent upper palace, vast gardens sloping downhill to the city and, along with several auxiliary buildings, a lower one-storey palace that marks the end of the gardens, was built by Prince Eugene of Savoy at the beginning of the eighteenth century. Because the upper palace offers a splendid view of the city, the complex was named Belvedere. Prince Eugene intended the upper palace, constructed later and one of the architect J. Lukas von Hildebrandt's masterworks, to serve as a representation of royal power and a venue for celebrations, invitations and other such occasions befitting one of Europe's wealthiest men, sharpest intellects and most ruthless military commanders. The lower palace was built as a summer residence. Only months after the grimacer of Beaune had cast his spell over me, did it suddenly occur to me that I had first encountered him in the Lower Belvedere.

Today the Austrian Gallery is housed in the Upper Belvedere and the collection of older paintings is exhibited in the lower palace. And it was there, when I was twenty, that I happened on him in a room that seemed to be reserved for him alone, the grimacer who had masqueraded as a Dutchman in Beaune and has been wandering the world under a variety of identities for more than 230 years. The room was dedicated to the Austrian sculptor Franz Xaver Messerschmidt's so-called character heads, which this initially celebrated court painter created in Bratislava between 1777 and 1783 after his academic career in Vienna had been destroyed by a certified 'confusion in the head'. Messerschmidt is believed to have produced sixty-nine of these 'head-pieces', as he called them, fifty five of which have been preserved. A number of them are on view in the Lower Belvedere.

These head-pieces—seventeen of alabaster and the rest mostly of metal—are busts that, for the most part, depict their human subjects frontally from the crown of the head roughly to the shoulder. What they show are the wildest grimaces in the history of art, faces contorted in ways never seen before, facial muscles straining against each other in anatomically possible but highly unlikely ways, deforming the subjects' countenances to frightening recognizability; a recognizability that offers no certainty because these faces with eyes wide open or spasmodically squeezed shut, lips pressed so firmly together that the effort causes the cheeks to swell curiously, chins jammed so forcefully onto the throats that they form unshapely bulges, and brows furrowed in dreadful grooves of pain—these faces, in short, while revealing nothing anatomically impossible, evidence an extreme anomalousness. And this has a peculiar, additionally irritating effect: since we have no everyday experience of mimetic extremism, we have no idea how to interpret these facial expressions and the busts later dubbed character heads leave us completely in the dark as to the characters of the persons portrayed.

This so unnerved Messerschmidt's contemporaries that they sought to have the artist, who had come to Vienna at nineteen in 1755 and was commissioned a few years later to create colossal bronze busts of Empress Maria Theresia and her husband Franz I. Stephan, declared an eccentric and freakish outcast. He was denied the professorship at the Academy of Fine Arts that had been promised to him because he had begun distancing himself from the perfect mastery of Baroque representational art. Instead, he was offered a tidy pension on the condition that he retire—he was not even forty years old. Messerschmidt gruffly declined the offer. He was no 'state artist' after all, even if he had gained enormous renown as one in his younger years and had received commissions for portrait busts and statues of counts and princes as well as marble sculptures of the Blessed Virgin Mary and John the Apostle, which can be seen in St Stephen's Cathedral. Messerschmidt left Vienna for Munich and then continued on to Bratislava, where he lived solely in pursuit of his artistic mission—widely considered the whim of a lunatic— of creating his head-pieces without any regard for the court and its official arbiters of taste.

Yet the latter were to follow him even there, where he died in 1783 not long after turning forty-seven. A few years after his death, an anonymous person drew up the first inventory list of the head-pieces and gave them the names they still bear today but which contribute nothing whatsoever to our understanding of them and their expressions or of Messerschmidt's work in general. At best the names detract from the characters they describe, but more often they counteract the gravity as well as the wit of Messerschmidt's portraits with a simple-minded pedantry that tries to cope with their mystery by assigning them titles like 'An Intentional Wag' or 'Afflicted with Constipation' or 'The Simpleton'.

On one of my first visits to Vienna, I ended up rather by chance in the gallery of the Lower Belvedere and then, inevitably, in the Messerschmidt room of grimacers where I lost my composure. The head-pieces I saw there made a simultaneously alarming and laugh-out-loud comical impression on me. This dual effect of alienation, that is, the paradoxical sense one gets when looking at these heads of being seized by contradictory emotions, seems to be inherent in the objects themselves and is the source of their energy.

The grimacer I would meet thirty years later in his natural habitat, as it were, albeit in the extremely cultivated habitat of a French restaurant, is the one in the Austrian Gallery called 'The Arch-villain.' At the time, I knew nothing about Messerschmidt, neither that he had left Vienna in disgust nor how posterity would try to pathologize his character heads—complete outliers and utterly unique in his time—an effort that essentially continues today. But even then, when I still thought the titles came from the artist himself, I was perplexed. I explained it away as a joke on the part of the sculptor because the 'Arch-villain', with his face contorted into a grimace replete with bulges and wrinkles, gave no evidence of the villainy announced in the title. Instead, to me, this dreadful bald head made of lead and tin with its violently contorted countenance expressed pain and distress, unbearable physical suffering and convulsive, self-contained emotional agony. When, after making a tour of the room, I returned to the 'Arch-villain' filled with a sense of astonished alienation, I was convinced that I perceived something utterly different in his swollen face: a hint of mockery, an expression of scorn almost completely hidden by his muscular spasm.

Since then, I have often come across pictures of the 'Arch-villain' and other Messerschmidt head-pieces in magazines, catalogues and books. And seeing them repeatedly in different contexts has confirmed my experience again and again: the character heads cannot be understood psychologically; they cannot be grasped through our repertoire of facial expressions; they unsettle precisely because they cannot be reduced to the characters they ostensibly display, nor to any character at all, for that matter, or any familiar feelings.

These faces always also contain the opposite of what they seem to express at first glance. And each of these heads is a spectacle of its own, in which conflicting characters struggle with each other, fight against each other—and merge with each other in a frightening, no, an outrageous way.

Soliman, the Mummified Enlightenment Thinker: An Addendum

Only a few years ago, a bust of Joseph Wenzel I, Prince of Liechtenstein, was identified as the work of Franz Xaver Messerschmidt. The Prince of Liechtenstein was not just any Austrian aristocrat. As Lord of the Liechtenstein Majorat, he commanded more than a million subjects and with all his latifundia, he was considered the wealthiest man in the Habsburg Monarchy. An enlightened despot, he did not hold with the wanton consumption of the feudal treasure he had inherited, but instead sought to use it productively and, by the standards of his era and position, to increase his wealth and properties efficiently through modern mercantilism. The bust Messerschmidt sculpted of him, probably a year before he left Vienna, shows the sculptor on his evolution from celebrated representational artist to the ostracized creator of the head-pieces.

Joseph Wenzel I is portrayed with astonishing naturalism and shown, like the later character heads, only from his head to his bare shoulders. He is depicted without his insignia of power, without the decorations of his status, as a confident old man with a narrow face ending in a sharp chin, raised eyebrows, an arched nose and broad, sensual lips, wearing an expression of sharp intelligence heightened with gentle scorn. Or rather, I should specify, he *seems* to be depicted—I specify, because Messerschmidt endowed this portrait bust, too, with an ambiguous, yes, equivocal expression that is difficult to grasp.

About ten years before Messerschmidt captured him for all eternity, Joseph Wenzel I had brought a man to Vienna to serve as his chamberlain and travelling companion. In this case 'valet' is in no way to be understood as a footman who empties his master's chamber pot or helps him dress or undress should the latter be too overwhelmed to manage on his own. Instead, this chamberlain was one of the closest confidants of his count, prince and emperor. His role was to be an advisor, as aware of what went on at court as of the mood among the populace, and so be in a position to offer advice his lord could not get from his royal peers and his salaried flatterers. This man was, moreover, an intellectual who was also aware of spiritual and philosophical currents, knowledge of which was forbidden by the authorities.

The chamberlain Angelo Soliman was so successful as a confidential advisor that not only was he entrusted with many tasks by his master and dispatched on sensitive missions but he also quickly became a popular figure throughout Vienna. The prince owes his legendary reputation as a generous benefactor of the beggars and the poor of Vienna not least to Soliman who knew how to direct the prince's eyes benevolently to things he would never have noticed, elevated as he was in his golden coach above the other high nobility to an almost monarchical status.

When Soliman had the audacity to wed a Viennese bourgeoise without asking his lord's permission, which surely would have been denied, Joseph Wenzel I unceremoniously relieved Soliman of his titles and banished him from the court. Yet immediately after the death of the prince, who was truly great not only in his beneficence but also in his rage, Soliman was reinstated to his position by Joseph Wenzel I's son. Soliman, fluent in several languages and an avowed supporter of the Enlightenment, became a member of the Masonic lodge 'True Harmony' in his later years. Beloved by the people and highly regarded in cultivated circles, Soliman died on 21 November 1796—and was stuffed and mummified the next day. Angelo Soliman was an African, after all, a Moor, as they were then called, who had been brought to Vienna enslaved.

His origins were wreathed with countless legends early on. He was said to be the son of an African king, a descendant of the ancient tribe of Numidians or of the Kanuri people who settled the area that would later become the border between Nigeria and Chad . . . All that is certain is that he was captured as a child by slave hunters and was then in the possession of various Europeans until he landed with a Sicilian countess who, noble as she was, made a present of him to Prince Lobkowitz, the Austrian governor of Sicily. From Lobkowitz he was handed over to the Prince of Liechtenstein and transferred from Sicily to Vienna. From enslaved man to princely advisor, from son of an African king to Viennese bourgeois husband, from Moor to Freemason: power takes many paths, this one led to Vienna.

Although he was highly respected and despite the high position he held when alive, Soliman was given to a taxidermist the day after his death against his daughter's adjurations and in defiance of the Archbishop of Vienna's Christian opposition. After being skinned and stuffed by an expert, his body was incorporated into the Imperial Natural History Collection as an odd piece of booty. There, those who had known him or those who had only heard about him could visit Soliman, half-naked and preserved as a noble animal for ten years. His stuffed body was then put in storage until it was destroyed in a fire in 1848 and the dead man, whose origins were never known, was finally allowed to disappear from the face of the earth.

Feuchtersleben: A Trail That Is False but Beautiful

In 1994, when I was overcome with a mysterious ailment for several months, a condition that led my friends to joke that I, who at that time was at my heaviest, would soon dwindle to nothing from the 'wasting disease' as it was called in old books, a friend visiting me in my sickbed presented me with one such book. He handed it to me with a touch of melancholy mockery, likely aimed at himself more than at me since he suffered much more often than I, a rank beginner, from unexpected slumps in energy and self-confidence, from which he managed, just as enigmatically, to emerge after a period of time. The book, written by Ernst von Feuchtersleben, an author I knew then only by name, was called *The Dietetics of the Soul* and this volume had appeared in its forty-sixth edition in 1886 from the Viennese publisher Carl Gerold's Sohn.

In an effort to dispel my boredom by reading this curious find, I began leafing through it. What the author understood as 'dietetics of the soul' are methods to preserve the soul's health. He was convinced that when the soul is at risk of becoming ill, it seeks some vexatious or painful ailment in the body in order to make its disease or endangerment known. Conversely, he believed that some despondency of mind could be dispelled through physical activity. As I read, I soon understood why so many of Feuchtersleben's contemporaries revered him as a life-teacher and soother of souls. 'A person is not always disposed to do everything,' I read, 'but he is always disposed to do something. This he should do.' Had this clever man in the mid-nineteenth century not spoken as if he were addressing me, who, at the end of the twentieth century, had fallen into an unfathomable apathy because for a long time I'd no longer want to do something I felt professionally obligated to? The book engaged me so completely that I stood up from my easy chair to get a pencil so I could underline sentences like the following (even though the life wisdom they contain, like all bits of life wisdom, does have petty-bourgeois aspects): 'To the curing of mental ailments, one's understanding brings nothing, reason little, time a great deal, resignation and activity everything.'

Period. Resignation—and activity then. But what is that? Passive activity, active resignation? Or what Thomas Mann would later call the ethos of endurance and perseverance and Jean Améry would even later call 'heroic nihilism'—in other words, carrying on in the knowledge that one's actions are futile? Be that as it may, a beautiful sentence can brighten your mood even when your intellect disagrees with it and your reason contradicts it and you believe that you are not free to wait for the healing effects of time. Not that Baron Ernst von Feuchtersleben's lucid thoughts immediately restored my strength, but I nevertheless resolved to engage more deeply with the author of this wonderfully consoling work when I was strong enough.

This is what I initially learnt about him. Born in 1806, Feuchtersleben was a writer and medical doctor who—hard to believe—had only started writing after he'd begun practicing medicine in Vienna and he and his wife found their childless existence difficult to cope with. Today, he is considered to be the great forefather of psychosomatics, which Viktor Frankl emphatically referred to, but as a writer he has disappeared into the footnotes in studies of Austrian Biedermeier literature.

What I learnt next appealed to me even more, probably because it ended up being a false trail. Feuchtersleben descended from a line of Austrian officers. His father, who had received a high medal for bravery in some Habsburg military campaign as a young man, fell in love with a highly cultivated, confident woman known as the 'beautiful mulatto of Vienna'. When he married Josefine Soliman two years after she had been unable to stop the exhibition of her mummified father, Ernst's father had to resign from his position as officer, take up engineering as a profession and move with his wife to Krakow.

The forefather of psychosomatics, the medical comforter of countless readers who could read in the pages of the many editions of *Dietetics* that bodily illnesses could be cured through the awareness of one's psychological entanglements and that mental suffering could be evaded through physical activity and socially meaningful work— did he have an African grandfather and an unprejudiced woman named Magdalena Cristiani for a grandmother? That would have suited me. Unfortunately, I learnt otherwise a few years later from a book about Feuchtersleben. Josefine Soliman, whose married name was von Feuchtersleben, bore her husband a son christened Eduard in Krakow and died not long after at the age of twenty-nine. The widower returned to Vienna, accompanied by his noticeably dark-complexioned young son and remarried. His second wife, Cäcilia von Clusolis bore him a son after a year, as his first wife had, named him Ernst and soon shared the fate of her predecessor, dying before the age of thirty.

How did the story end? Not at all well. The twice-widowed father took his own life in the Danube in 1834. Still, his older son Eduard, Angelo Soliman's grandson, did become an honourable engineer who directed the salt mines in Ausseerland. An engraving shows him as a man attractive in a feminine way with features that would later have been called pronouncedly Black. And what about

Ernst von Feuchtersleben, who not only assiduously proclaimed the human right to happiness but also ascribed to humanity the ability to achieve personal happiness through self-discipline and recommended 'resignation and activity' as the appropriate defence against the eternal allure of sadness? He made it to the age of forty-three and died a difficult death after a long illness.

His entire doctrine of how to keep the soul healthy and cure the body through psychological self-awareness evolved on the edge of an abyss into which Ernst von Feuchtersleben had looked early on and of which he was aware his entire life: 'A dreadful seed of insanity sleeps in the mind of every man. Use all your powers of good cheer and activity to ensure that it never wakes!' The grimacer of Beaune was fully aware of this seed and knew it lurked inside him, ready to sprout, and it would have been interesting to discuss Messerschmidt's character heads with him, busts he had surely never seen. They would not have appealed to him since he was almost desperate in his regard for the moderation and self-control with which humans can achieve cheerful inner harmony, but which in Messerschmidt's heads became a cramp-inducing compulsive harmony.

Ungargasse 5: A Postscript

The literary renown of Ungargasse in Vienna's third district comes from the fact that Ingeborg Bachmann set her novel *Malina* on this street and in the surrounding 'Ungargassenland' with topographical precision, and even though it becomes a deadly setting for the narrator, it has gained an almost utopian homeland characteristic. 'But Washington and Moscow and Berlin are merely impertinent places putting on airs of self-importance,' the narrator says near the beginning. 'In my Ungargassenland no one takes them seriously or people just smile at their importunities as at the declarations of ambitious upstarts . . .' The narrator lives at Ungargasse 6 and her lover Ivan lives at 'Number 9 with the two bronze lions at the entrance'—less practically than tormentingly close. The long street which runs from Heumarkt to Rennweg—and past the Lower Belvedere with the Austrian Gallery—is described several times by the narrator on her way to the city or when she is once again fleeing from herself and her unconditional desire. Mostly she praises Ungargasse because it offers everything necessary for city life—a few inns and small cafes along with a pharmacy, newsstand and bakery—and at the same time it lacks anything that might make it an attraction for tourists who hardly ever come there. The street gets its name from the merchants who, having come to Vienna from Hungary with their horses and wagons, would stop in one of the street's many hostels, just as Ivan, the lover who is unable to offer Bachmann's narrator the radical devotion she desperately demands and tests, has come to Vienna from Hungary.

In the winter of 2007, I spent a week in Vienna taking care of a few things that could only resolved in the capital and yet found enough time between my obligations to become bored in my hotel, so I set out one afternoon to take a look at Ungargasse, which I had not visited since my first trip to Vienna a long time before. I entered the street from Rennweg, where it opens onto a very active, rather chaotic intersection. Any visitor who strolls along the gently downward sloping street with Bachmann's novel in mind will find much of Ungargasse as she described it with small shops and certain stretches with a small-town atmosphere despite the heavy traffic. Then the visitor will notice that the 'offensive innovations' the author wrote about in 1971 have aged considerably and been outdone by far coarser offences.

Diagonally across from the 'Alter Heller' inn, which Bachmann mentions time and again as if it were part of her 'Ungargassenland' charm, I noticed an unspectacular house on the other side of the street that is—I would almost add oddly enough—not mentioned in *Malina* and bears a commemorative plaque: 'Petar Preradović. 1818–1872. The great Croatian poet.' Like Ivan, one of the two men in Ingeborg Bachmann's novel, Petar Preradović came to Vienna a foreigner and, like Malina, the book's second, eponymous male character who works in the Museum of Military History, he came from Croatia and had something to do with the Imperial and Royal Army. In fact, Preradović achieved the rank of general despite his dislike of the military profession. In addition, like both the novel's narrator and its author, Petar Preradović, who lived across the street from the inn extolled in *Malina*, wrote poetry—primarily love poems but also patriotic verse that does not glorify nationalist arrogance but instead combines patriotism, democracy, concern for the many who were disenfranchised and kept in ignorance and the pathos of world brotherhood.

Preradović was born in a Dalmatian village and educated in the military schools of the Habsburg army. By the age of twenty, after all the drills in garrison towns, he had forgotten his mother tongue. He rediscovered it in Milan, of all places, where he was stationed for a long time and which had an old connection to Zadar and Dalmatia. As an adult he reacquired the language he had been robbed of in childhood and in just a few years he was writing the most nuanced Croatian of his time. He believed the Balkan Slavs would finally be able to lead Europe into an era of eternal peace. In an ode entitled 'Slavjanstvu', he invokes Slavdom as a liberating and unifying force for the coming age. These are unusual poems for an Austrian general as much for their proclamation of peace and freedom as for the pathos of a South Slavic awakening. His verse epic 'Prvi ljudi' (The First People)—like *Malina*—is about love and asks if love and reason, passion and rationality can ever be united. When Adam, lost in his paradise, sees himself reflected in the water, he becomes aware of his loneliness and in despair calls on his Creator to complete his work and 'give my "I" a companion like me', whereupon God creates woman not from Adam's rib but from another particle of dust.

It is curious that Ingeborg Bachmann, who scattered quite a few references to 'Ungargassenland' in her novel, made no mention Petar Preradović. But perhaps she was not aware of him and when she was writing her book, the building at Ungargasse 39 did not yet have the plaque it now bears, the plaque that would no longer be possible to mount since its call to remember the great Croatian poet—one who dreamt of Slavs in the Balkans as bringers of peace to the new Europe—is sponsored by an institution that no longer exists; it was swept away in streams of blood and only survives in Vienna on a rusting plaque on the Ungargasse: The Yugoslavian Academy of Arts and Sciences.

The winter of 2007 was the warmest in human memory and in many Austrian ski resorts the ski lifts were closed. Even individuals markedly prone to sugar-coating discovered they could make waves as apocalyptic prophets of global warming and because it was so unusually warm for weeks on end, thousands of Austrians came down with cold. I, too, suffered the usual symptoms and when it started to rain, I sought shelter. I found it across the street from the inconspicuous Number 6 in a single-storey corner building slightly reminiscent of a country house that was called the Beer Devil: Bierteufel. The Inn of One Hundred Beers. It was late afternoon when I stepped into the room that had been steeped in the cigarette smoke of several generations. I noticed right away that only a few of the tables were occupied and I would be the only one drinking alone. The other afternoon boozers sat at their tables in groups of two or four. Overwhelmed by the choice of a hundred different beers, I ordered one brewed by a privately-owned Styrian brewery I had never heard of and stepped out of the inn to check a signage I had only glanced at when hurrying inside. Yes, Number 5 on Ungargasse was the so-called Beethoven House—one of the countless Beethoven houses in Vienna, it must be said—and this one's claim to fame was that the composer had completed his Ninth Symphony here.

I then drank a Slovakian beer, which the waiter, who was perhaps himself Slovakian, seemed to slam onto my table with particular satisfaction. I was in the 'Beer Devil', there was no doubt, and after I'd been sitting at my table drinking for a while, I got the feeling I was being covertly examined by the drinkers at the neighbouring tables. I decided to flee the devil, who, as I knew all too well, was also in me. I paid and went out into the rain. On the Beatrixgasse side of the building with the two Beethoven plaques near its front door on Ungargasse, was mounted a third plaque which read: 'In this house lived and died Ján Kollár. 1849–1852. Professor and Slovakian poet. Donated by the Slovakians of Vienna.'

Of course, Ján Kollár, as his name is most often spelt, lived longer than just three years, but he did spend his three final years in Vienna in precisely this house. There is much to be said about him, but even a book about stray paths is not required to follow every byway to its end, especially since there would be no end, given that each stray path would only lead me to another and yet another. But when I was writing down my memories of the grimacer of Beaune and following the paths that would lead me from a restaurant in Burgundy to this Viennese inn at Ungargasse 5 a few years later, I found the notes I had collected on Messerschmidt, a biographical report that until then had seemed completely irrelevant.

When Messerschmidt still enjoyed the Prince's favour in Vienna and believed he could live a respectable life as sculptor, he purchased a large house or small palais with the money he'd earned from his head-pieces. It served him at once as a residence, a workshop and a storehouse for his sculptures. It was there, at Ungargasse 5, the Beethoven and Kollár house, that I'd escaped the beer devil, at least on that mild early-summerlike evening in February 2007.

CHAPTER TWO

Liberation Boulevard: Belgrade

We hadn't counted on meeting the friendliest of all Europeans, worldly big-city dwellers whose urbane nature was one of unobtrusive helpfulness, in Belgrade of all places. When passers-by saw a foreigner absorbed in a map and the far from simple task of matching the Cyrillic names on street signs with the Latin counterparts on the map, they often stopped and offered to help. As soon as they finished their explanation, they said goodbye and continued on their way. After a few days it seemed to me that this unobtrusive helpfulness was not a particular trait you can find in certain people everywhere but a trait of Belgrade itself. Or, at least, those unfortunate traits that seem innate to many residents of major cities, did not appear to be at all widespread among the residents of the historical neighbourhoods: Dorćol, Stari Grad, Palilula, Vračar or Savski Venac. Whether they were queuing in stores or driving in a long line of cars, they rarely displayed the self-centeredness of hurried city-slickers with their inevitable sense of being lone warriors and if anyone did become pushy and try to cut ahead, either in his car or in the queue, he stood out as the disconcerting exception.

We had checked into Hotel Moskva, a large, five-storey building often shown in views of Belgrade. It was built in 1907 in a kind of eastern European Jugendstil-style and still has its original chiselled facade of tiles, yellow Majolica discs and green faience ornaments. The hotel stands on Terazije Square, an extensive plaza or, rather, the end of a street in the dead centre of the city, an area pulsing night and day with both life and death. Centuries ago, the Turks favoured this square for a series of hangings when they wanted to cow those of their Serbian subjects who were no longer willing to submit to Turkish rule, and as soon as the National Socialists captured Belgrade they, too, hanged Serbian patriots from the lampposts of Terazije.

Yet many demonstrations against state authorities also began here and in March 1991 workers and students kept watch at the tall, slender fountain in front of the hotel to keep the sleep of reason from spreading over their city. Nevertheless, a few weeks later spectres of nationalism ruled Belgrade and chased out those who had tried to defend their city's free spirit. Military police patrols hunted down young men in the streets, dragged them off to the barracks and from there sent them to a war they never would have joined on their own. I wondered if any of the people we encountered as we made our way through this city, astonished by the residents' friendliness, had been among those scared away by those spectres or had been spectres themselves.

In the 1930s, the central committee of the Zenitists, a group of avant-garde artists, met in Hotel Moskva. Later, too, it would always be more than a hotel: the seat of various literary circles, a meeting place for political groups and, still today, for Montenegrin business-men. The hotel seemed, meanwhile, to be capitalizing on its thread-bare elegance. The dimly lit landings one stepped into from the lift were enormous on every floor, the long hallways were carpeted with plush dark-red rugs, the rooms were spacious, the wallcoverings colourful, the upholstery substantial. But when I pulled the door closed energetically behind me, the knob came off in my hand, and a thin stream of water ran ceaselessly from the bathtub faucet whether the tap was turned on or off. The entire hotel was a stage that had lost its ensemble and audience, but the backdrops remained and a small group of actors had returned to pretend we were guests in a glamorous hotel of yesteryear, having arrived in the 1920s, at just the right time to experience the era of the cosmopolitan, ecstatically decadent Belgrade. Or we found ourselves in the 70s, in a Yugoslavia respected throughout the world, with people visiting from all over the globe since the country had initiated the Non-Aligned Movement and Belgrade was considered its global capital. We were both spectators at a daily performance that paid homage to the myth of the old Belgrade and the vanished Yugoslavia and minor characters in the performance.

We had set off from the hotel into the pedestrian zone but soon branched off the overcrowded Kneza Mihailova Street, where international fashion chains have their branches, leftwards into a neighbourhood of buildings that were relatively old by Belgrade standards. The city does not have many buildings left that reflect its eventful history. The fact that there is no old construction testifies to the historical fate of a city often conquered and destroyed. The poet Vasko Popa viewed his hometown as 'white bones', as bones shooting out of the 'ploughed burial grounds'. In one gently curved street, Topličin Venac, we realized that diagonally across from the once famous Palace Hotel, we had stumbled on the house of Platon Papakostopoulos, which one of the actors at the reception desk had told us about. Papakostopoulos, a brilliant man born in 1864, was well suited to the Belgrade we were attuned to in Hotel Moskva. He was Greek, although the encyclopedia of medical history describes him as the founder of Serbian pediatrics. His first language was Greek but he was granted an honorary seat in a side loge of Serbian literary history because he devoted what limited hours of leisure he had as Belgrade's first pediatrician to a complete verse translation of the *Odyssey* and the *Iliad* from ancient Greek into new Serbian, standardized a generation earlier with a definitive grammar and spelling by the language reformer Vuk Karadžić.

Traces of Vuk Karadžić are everywhere in Belgrade even though he only lived there for a few years and spent decades in Vienna. From Topličin Venac to the right, it is only a few steps to the Orthodox cathedral. You would expect to see a church with a Baroque tower like this in a Lower Austrian village or in the pious Polish provinces. One of Belgrade's peculiarities is that this modest, inconspicuous cathedral in the city centre makes no more fuss than a random country church whereas the gigantic Church of Saint Sava can be seen from almost any point in the city because this monstrous architectural fraud, crowned with a massive dome, sits enthroned on a hill. To the left of the St Michael's Cathedral entrance lies the gravestone of Vuk Karadžić, to the right lies that of his teacher Dositej Obradović who wanted to free the Serbians' spiritual life from church and monastery but was nevertheless buried next to a cathedral entrance. Vuk Karadžić died in Vienna in 1864 and was buried in the St Marx Cemetery. On the centenary of his birth, his remains were relocated to Belgrade and reburied with national pomp.

Another day we walked through Dorćol, an old neighbourhood with a system of perpendicular alleys and tree-lined streets designed according to a plan that had been methodically implemented by the Habsburgs when they ruled Belgrade for a short period in the eighteenth century. The entire district slopes gently downhill to the city centre until it reaches the overgrown tracks of an abandoned railway line and behind it, the Danube. In Dorćol, first the Turks set up their caravanserai, which was then demolished by the Austrians. Their houses and palaces were in turn demolished by the Turks, all of whose mosques save one were demolished by the Serbs. Not far from the Bajrakli Mosque, which survived all the upheavals, including attacks by Serbian nationalists who wanted to crown their fight against the Bosnian Muslims with a symbolic heroic exploit by burning down their city's sole religious monument from the Ottoman era, we once again came across Vuk or Wolf Karadžić. The Great Academy of Belgrade, founded as a *grande école*, was the first Serbian institution in which the nation's youth were taught the ideals of the Enlightenment and was housed in a building designed in the style of an Ottoman manor. Dositej Obradović taught here, confident that the rays of the Western Enlightenment would also illuminate the Balkans. And it was here that his student Vuk Karadžić became convinced that the Enlightenment had to shine in the East of its own accord.

Two taxis stood in front of the closed university. A large chessboard was set up in the open trunk of the first car and because only a few pieces were left on the board one of the drivers asked if we would allow him time to finish the match which he seemed to be losing. When the match was over and we were sitting in the taxi, he wanted to know why we were interested in the Great Academy and when I told him he asked if he could make a small detour. He drove past the Hotel Moskva and took the road that led to the longest street in the city, Bulevar Kralja Aleksandra, along both sides of which trams rumbled by on ancient tracks. He drove past the completely gutted Hotel Metropole, where the delegations of the Non-Aligned states had met forty years ago, past two classical university buildings and the university library, then he spun the steering wheel sharply, stopped on the edge of a small park, and looked at us expectantly.

On a pedestal 3-metre high, sat a delicate man with an enormous moustache, a rustic hat on his head and an open book on his right knee: Vuk, the driver said, nodding as if he had not merely driven us to a monument that seemed to be a meeting place for the students of the nearby institutions and people from the neighbourhood, but had found the key to the museum and shown us the books and possessions of a man with whom he had an intimate connection. I was astonished at first and then delighted that many Serbs, when they talked about the great figures of their history, called them only by their first names, like the taxi driver who referred to the erudite Karadžić so familiarly as Vuk that one could be excused for thinking he was talking about a deceased relative.

It was our fifth day in the city, and we were busy with a few matters in Hotel Moskva before we finally set out from the execution site to the site of liberation. The Bulevar Kralja Aleksandra is not the most beautiful street in Belgrade, but it is one of the most interesting in Europe. If you walk through it from beginning to end, from Terazije Square to the Church of Saint Sava, you pass all the stations of Serbian history like the Stations of the Cross. Naturally, there is also, right at the start, a building dedicated to the Father of the Nation, a building that elegantly replaces the Jugendstil with an historically allusive style and houses the Vuk Karadžić Foundation which provides grants to young scholars and artists. On the other side of the boulevard, quite near its beginning, the Old and the New

Palaces face each other warily. The Obrenović kings ruled in the former and in the latter ruled the Karadjordjević, two dynasties that superseded each other several times over the course of the nineteenth century. The row of representative edifices is interrupted by a small street that leads to a quiet park. Here stands the life-sized monument to Ivo Andrić, a Belgradian of the old Yugoslavian variety given that his mother tongue was Croatian, he grew up in Bosnian Travnik and lived most of his life in Belgrade, a stone's throw from the boulevard of Serbian history. From his apartment in a corner building, we looked down on the lovely park with the spreading canopies of old trees and I recalled a character from one of Andrić's stories in a collection I had edited a few years earlier: a weary professor who would always stretch out on a bench under a tree in a park very much like this one in order to recapture, in the rustling of the leaves, the feeling he had had in his childhood of sitting in the roaring sea and basking in the aching delight of self-forgetfulness.

Along the Bulevar Kralja Milana, you find everything that testifies to Serbian history and its contradictions: the palaces of the rival royal dynasties which bestowed on the Serbs in the nineteenth century many unenlightened and despotic kings, hardly any of whom died of natural causes or avoided being stabbed, shot or blown to pieces by a bomb; the street, the public park and the house of the writer who recounted with unbiased rage and the empathetic balance of an epic poet of antiquity all the horrors inflicted on the Yugoslavian people and those they inflicted on each other; Belgrade in its bourgeois era with the 1906 Donau-Adria Savings Bank and merchant houses built in the Secession style, though with an oddly patriotic twist, sometimes even painted in the red, blue and white colours of the Serbian flag, like the quirky house facing the flower market

... and socialist Modernism with the nearly black, more than 100-metre-tall high-rise, built in the 1960s and exuberantly nicknamed the Beograđanka, the Belgrade Lady, formerly a showpiece of socialist department stores, now a shabby epitaph to a vanished epoch when they still believed in Communism, in the unity of the peoples, in Yugoslavia. During the Yugoslav Wars, Studio B92 was based in the Beograđanka. It was the only opposition broadcaster in that era of nationalism—when the guardians of tradition destroyed the inheritance they invoked—that the government did not shut down...

After about 3 kilometres, the boulevard opens onto Slavija Square. This is an enormous, aggressive behemoth of an intersection, roughly 300-metre wide, into which six large roads flow, feeding hundreds of cars into the roundabout each minute in a stream that moves jerkily around the star-shaped course before they are spun out again. The square is ugly, without form and lined with unattractive, badly designed buildings—and it pulses with life all day, all night, all year long. On the northern edge sits a massive building with a glass facade that reflects Hotel Slavia where the Socialist Workers' Party of Yugoslavia was founded more than eighty years ago. Today this political party must take care to keep from collapsing like the nation for which grandiose plans had been debated in this hotel.

On the other side of Slavia Square, the boulevard grows calm. Trees line both sides of this gently ascending road. Now that we were so close to the Church of Saint Sava, the goal on which we had had our eyes fixed for the entire way, we could no longer see it—at least not until we climbed the small hill and saw it rise dauntingly before us. Sava, the patron saint of Serbia, died almost 800 years ago and yet he lives on not only in the believers' prayers but also in their grief and rage. With great emotion, they kiss the icons that depict him, in which they believe he is present. They still weep for him and renew their devotion to him each year in commemoration of the terrible fate he suffered when the Ottoman Grand Vizier had his bones exhumed more than four centuries ago and, according to the legend, ordered them defiled and incinerated on this very hill. He wanted the flames to rise high enough for the rebels in Banat, on the other side of the Danube, to see them. With this heinous act, the Grand Vizier had intended to break their pride and determination.

In 1894, 300 years after this profanation was inflicted on the Serbs, the cornerstone for the largest Orthodox church was laid at this very place to commemorate for all eternity the ignominy they suffered and to remind them that redemption entailed first and foremost the restoration of their national dignity. Still, decades passed before a church was built in which a mass could be celebrated. Its dimensions were so vast that only the foundations had been laid when the National Socialists, who wanted to break the spiritual strength of the conquered land, forbade further construction. And after the Second World War, the Orthodox community in communist Yugoslavia was not allowed to resume construction. Only in 1985, almost 100 years after the cornerstone was laid, were builders summoned to resume work on the church of the national patron saint. The times seemed propitious for a church dedicated to not just anyone but to the Serbian patron saint on whose bones the Muslims had committed sacrilege.

But it was not a church from 1985 nor one from 1894 that made us dizzy when we raised our eyes to gaze at the massive dome, but one from the sixth century. What the Byzantines achieved with Hagia Sophia, from which the Church of Saint Sava copied its architectural dimensions, has not succeeded here. To be sure, the magnificent outer walls are finally complete and thanks to great technical efforts, the dome was set upon the walls and a 12-metre-tall gold cross was mounted ᴏn top of the dome. Inside, however, the delicate work on the mosaics and frescos is still far from complete and here and there the extravagant church has begun to crumble. Those at work here are architects of ruins and no matter how self-sacrificingly they labour, they cannot keep up with the deterioration they themselves cause. The dimensions of this church constructed in the style of the sixth century with twenty-first century materials are so gigantic that as soon as one part is properly finished, another falls apart, and no matter how fast the builders work, they will never catch up to the sixth century. And no matter how ardently the believers—of which 12,000 can fit in the church—entreat the miracle-working Sava, whom the enemy mistreated outrageously even in death, they do not find the deliverance they desire today.

As we were leaving the Church of Saint Sava, lightning flashed in the distant banks of black clouds. The entire city seemed surrounded by a constant rumbling but the cathartic storm did not break that night. We sat up late in the garden of a restaurant on French street, the Francuska. Thousands of gnats swirled around the guests whose faces and arms were covered with inflamed red bumps but they paid no attention to the insects. We sat in the garden, listening to an articulate waiter instructing us with shy sincerity that it was very unjust to identify Serbia with nationalism and war because its people longed for the wider world and for peace with it.

The Invention of Yugoslavia in Vienna:
And an Excursion to Jasenovac

In Vienna's third district, Marokkanergasse, Moroccan Street— almost directly across from the Lower Belvedere, where I once encountered the inscrutable Messerschmidt's grimaces—leads down to the Heumarkt. It was on this street that Vuk Karadžić, the father of the Serbian nation, lived for more than fifty years after arriving in Vienna as a twenty-seven-year-old refugee.

Having grown up in a remote village in western Serbia, he did not have the advantage of any higher education. And yet in Vienna, in just a few years and as if from thin air, he managed to lay the foundations for the Serbian nation: he standardized the popular language, established a new grammar and orthography, and collected folk tales, songs and poems that had until then only been transmitted orally. In creating the standardized language, he defied the threat of excommunication and turned away from Church Slavonic, which no one understood, and proposed instead a clever balance of the different dialects spoken in each town. His new system of grammar, intended to be easily taught and learned, followed the principle of 'write the way you talk and read what is written', which entailed subverting the traditional orthography that made reading and writing a secret science reserved for the elite. And just as the Brothers Grimm collected German folk tales, Karadžić gathered the Serbians' folk literature, preserving its riches from an earlier age for a new era.

In his first year in Vienna, Vuk Karadžić met the two people who would change the course of his life: the Slovenian scholar Jernej Kopitar and Anna Krauß, a young woman from suburban Vienna. Kopitar, an unfathomably gifted farmer's son who was sent to study in Vienna, published *Grammar of Slavic Languages in Carniola,*

Carinthia and Styria at the age of twenty-six. Called a 'monstrum scientarium' by his contemporaries, this monster of knowledge and erudition was engaged in the Imperial Court Library as custodian of all Slavic books. He taught Karadžić the fundamentals of philology which enabled the latter to do with Serbian what Kopitar had tried to do with Slovenian, that is, to develop a set of rules from the spoken language for an accessible standard written language. Kopitar also introduced him to Friedrich Schlegel, Jakob Grimm and the other German prophets of European vernaculars and folk literature who saw in him their Balkan prophet, whose arrival they had been ardently awaiting.

Anna Krauß offered the frail foreigner with a limp something else, namely, her heart, a home and, over the years, twelve children. Even in old age, when he was renowned throughout Europe, a member of academies across the continent, granted a pension by the Russian czar and every scientific honour the Austrian emperor had to bestow, Karadžić still complained that his wife was forced to endure such bitter poverty at his side. He had produced his grammar book of the Serbian language, a large Serbian dictionary with 27,000 definitions and his collection of folk songs which gave rise to a Serbian mode all over Europe, similar to the Greek mode, to which so many rebels paid tribute in liberal salons and every now and again on the battlefield. He had also managed to impose language reform in short order and despite great resistance. Nonetheless, he lived for many years in dire misery in a small apartment on Marokkanergasse without a secure income and surrounded by a growing horde of children periodically decimated by illnesses that thrived in the confined and damp living conditions of the time. Only two of their twelve children survived: one was Minna, the multilingual, erudite daughter who faithfully served her father as secretary and colleague, almost forgetting to live her own life and write her own books in the process.

Not far from Marokkanergasse, the much wider and longer Ungargasse leads from Rennweg towards the city centre. Here lived the Croatian general and poet Petar Preradović in the building that bears the unusual plaque I discovered by chance two years earlier. The plaque's dedication from the 'Yugoslavian Academy of Arts and Sciences' testifies to a country that foundered in blood but survives in Vienna, of all places, where that country had also, in a certain sense, been invented. And here, on this street in the third district, Vuk Karadžić and the younger Petar Preradović, the pioneer of modern Croatian literature, met for the first time. They became friends. After all, they wanted the same thing; for them language was not a tool for keeping people apart but for bringing them together.

Jernej Kopitar, who spent his days and nights poring over books in the Court Library, believed he had discovered that all Slavic languages were variants of a single, common, original language spoken by the Slavs. However, this conviction did not induce him to condemn the smaller languages to extinction and bet on a single, shared pan-Slavic tongue. Instead, it caused him to recognize the value and dignity of even the smallest languages, and inspired him to dream of a brilliant, fraternal future for all Slavs. It was also in Vienna that the Serbs and Croats discovered they shared a common language and here of all places, against whose rule the Slavic nations would later rise up, that they agreed their common language should have two different written variants. Delighted with all these awakenings to a bright future, Petar Preradović, the pacifist poet-general who rediscovered the maternal language he had been robbed of as a cadet in the Habsburg military academy in Milan, believed that none other than the fraternal nations of Croatia and Serbia would bring eternal peace to Europe and would never let themselves be divided.

In that hot summer when we had set off to explore Serbia, after leaving Belgrade, we exited the highway about 100 kilometres south-east of Zagreb. No sign on the Croatian road indicated that there was a place here named Jasenovac. The rural road led through a marshy area over which flocks of large birds circled and along vast fields under a scorching sun. Suddenly we glimpsed a 10-metre-tall stone flower, an enormous concrete lily bud blooming in the middle of a field. Here, between 1941 and 1945, had stood the Jasenovac concentration camp, built by the Ustaše-led fascist Croatian state, in which Jews, Orthodox priests, Muslims, Serbians, Roma, Communists of all nationalities as well as Croatians who had resisted the murderous regime were killed. There were no exits off the road. Instead, it led us around the field with the monument designed by the architect Bogdan Bogdanović, which from a distance looked intimidating rather than shocking, and on to the village a kilometre's distance from the camp.

An oppressive silence hung over the village, which was unusually densely built since every other house appeared bullet-ridden and uninhabited—and right next these decrepit buildings, their owners had built new homes, most with still unplastered red-brick walls. A small, blue kiddie pool filled with plastic ducks and all manner of toys stood in the garden of one recently built house, but on the other side of the neighbour's dilapidated wooden fence brambles were growing rampant through the front door of the abandoned house; here, pots of brightly coloured flowers were attractively arranged on the windowsill, and there, the branches of a tree growing inside the house were protruding between the roof beams. The Ustaše had kept a killing machine running on the municipal grounds of Jasenovac and, fifty years later, this village became a theatre of war. The fields surrounding the former camp became the deployment zone of enemy troops and the shabby village itself, home to 2,000 residents—some Serbian, others Croatian—was the prize over which the battle was fought.

When Croatia declared independence in 1991, Serbians, of whom over half a million had lived in the region of Krajina for centuries and therefore on Croatian territory, proclaimed the 'Republic of Serbian Krajina' and seceded from the newly established state. The Serb population in the historical regions of Baranja and Slavonia aligned themselves with their compatriots and as a result almost one third of the Croatian territory was under the control of a Serbian proto-state. The occupying forces of Jasenovac—located at the confluence of the Una and Sava rivers in southern Slavonia, once the breadbasket of Croatia—alternated every few months between the Yugoslav People's Army, which had long functioned as a Serbian national force, and the Croatian National Guard. Special forces on one side and on the other conquered the area and this village. The ethnic cleansing perpetrated by Serbian organizations that destroyed the Catholic church in Jasenovac and 200 other churches in the region was followed by the recapturing of the area by Croatian militiamen who in turn blew up the houses owned by Serbian inhabitants before they were dispelled again only to return a few months later, causing several more thousand people whose families had lived here for generations to flee. A number of commanding officers of the enemy militias who had ordered ethnic cleansing, abuse, torture, the murder of prisoners and the destruction of houses and churches in Krajina and Slavonia now sit peacefully in Swedish or Dutch prisons and spend their days playing chess or table tennis with each other and pining for Yugoslavian cuisine. The rank and file of the great massacre, however, have returned to what is called normal life in their towns and villages, murderers who killed after business hours or on holiday and are once again respectable citizens who perhaps dream every now and then of their next holiday.

We crossed the silent village, and the only signs of residents were tools left in gardens and tattered flags hanging from windows. The street led to the cemetery, but Jasenovac itself seemed to be a graveyard inhabited by suspicious people. After we had passed houses with broken windows, collapsed roofs and bullet holes in their facades as well as new buildings that looked strangely temporary, I noticed a small sign indicating that we were on the Ulica Petra Preradovića, or the street, here in this area of ethnic divisiveness, that was dedicated to the man who had preached enthusiastically that eternal peace between nations would spread around the world from a brotherhood of Serbs and Croats. At the cemetery we saw that, in truth, there were two separate graveyards in this small village: an Orthodox one that was large and well-cared-for and a Catholic one that was hardly presentable and in which the dead were apparently remembered with very little affection. In the new buildings lived Croats, whose houses had been destroyed by their Serbian neighbours, and Serbs, whose houses had been destroyed by their Croatian neighbours. They lived together again, as they always had, alongside their demolished former homes in view, and they buried their dead in two different cemeteries that had always faced each other and had always been accessed by Petar Preradović Street.

When we left the village, we came upon an unpaved road that led out to the field in which stood the renowned cement flower.

Even from a distance I had wondered anxiously if it weren't too large and imposing, and my reservations did not diminish as we came closer. But it wasn't the monument's disproportionate size that was appalling and upsetting on this site of commemoration, but the fact that everything here had been profanely left to ruin, the wooden-plank path on which we approached the monument and the memorial itself. The six wells from which Bogdan Bogdanović had this flower—a powerful symbol of grief—grow were empty, the stone petals were chipped, and here and there cracks in the masonry had been filled with silicone or coarsely plastered and roughly painted over. This monument, built in memory of the largest extermination site in the Balkans, would be forgotten and the memory of the Ustaše state and its crimes erased.

In the 1980s, however, a battle was fought for memory. At the time, Serbian and Croatian politicians, historians and propagandists were engaged in battles of words over Jasenovac, battles which would one day be fought with weapons. Serbian nationalists proclaimed Jasenovac the 'greatest Serbian city under the earth' and, as if there hadn't already been enough people killed, stabbed, shot or dead of hunger and disease, the number of victims kept swelling, the closer the bloody dissolution of the common state loomed until the writer and politician Vuk Drašković claimed that over a million Serbs had been murdered, an absurd count that was almost as high as the total number of victims of all Yugoslavian nationalities in the entire Second World War. In contrast, the number of victims in Croatian studies, which bore shameless titles like 'The Jasenovac Lie', steadily decreased until the extermination camp was transformed into a detention site that was an unavoidable consequence of the war, in which a few thousand people, the majority of whom were Croatian, regrettably lost their lives. The independent Simon Wiesenthal Center's estimate of 90,000 victims enraged both sides equally, the one side insisting the number was far too low if the dead were only Serbs, while the other side rejected the number of dead of all nationalities and religions because they knew the perpetrators were Croatians.

We drove back to the highway and headed towards the border that divided the Croats and Serbs. The ethnicization of anti-fascism was an important stage on the path to war and even today, years after the devastating war, it still prevents many Croats and Serbs from acknowledging crimes committed on their behalf and from recognizing the suffering of others because in this way fascists can always condemn the other nation's putative national character while claiming humanism as their own nation's eternal vested right.

Cars were backed up at the heavily fortified border. In her novel *Pave und Pero* (1940), the Austrian writer and granddaughter of Croatia's national poet, Paula von Preradović, now remembered only for having composed the text for the Austrian national anthem, depicted a meeting between Vuk Karadžić and Petar Preradović, in which they sit together in the poet general's apartment in Vienna's third district. The elderly Karadžić was visiting Preradović, pleased as he was about the changing times that were constantly improving and about the future that seemed to promise a happy era of freedom and peace, in order to say to the younger with a sense of emphatic friendship, 'But you see, Brother, that poets are already standing up and writing poetry in this, our language, whether you call it Serbian as I do or Croatian as you do. You see, Brother, it makes me so happy, that I had to come see you . . .'

CHAPTER THREE

The Wide World of Dragatuš: At Home with
Oton Župančič

It was about seven in the evening and in the dusk we had almost driven past Dragatuš. The Croatian border couldn't be far; the dull grey of a warm, rain-soaked day had become the glowing grey of a cool evening that brightened westward and promised lovely weather in the morning. We had come from the north, from Rog, the massive karstified plateau in the Gottschee, whose ancient forests had once been cleared by settlers from East Tyrol and Carinthia. In the forest of history, nature had long ago reclaimed the villages the Gottscheer had had to abandon during the Second World War. The town squares and fields, the orchards and roads they had begun clearing from the woods over 600 years ago were now covered again, six decades after their forced emigration, with dark, impenetrable forests. In a thicket, we came upon stone stairs that no longer led to any structure and crumbling masonry that had once lined a garden and property but was now overgrown with shrubbery.

It's easy to drive past Dragatuš, 30 or 40 kilometres to the south. You have to notice the small sign on the highway between Črnomelj and Vinica pointing only at a cornfield and then give in to the urge to drive into it. After about 300 metres, you arrive in a sprawling village that is lively into the evening hours with a monstrous conglomeration of buildings in its centre. A number of commercial buildings have been built around the core of an old tavern: the Supermercat Rina, the Pension Rina, the Župančičev hram Guest House. Rina—that was, no doubt, the fifty-year-old woman with the rather hefty torso in the taproom whose mere presence seemed to enforce a level of civility among the half-dozen men in tracksuits and slippers or coveralls and mud-spattered rubber boots whom she was serving beer and schnaps. The room was lit only by the twilight outside and a dim lamp hanging from the ceiling; two men sitting outside the circle of light were smoking in near darkness. All talk stopped when we entered, so Katharina Stefanić looked up, curious. We didn't even have a chance to ask if we could have a room for the night and a bite to eat, before she announced that a room was available on the second floor and the last dinner orders would be taken in half an hour.

From the room's balcony we could see the dark outline of the Rog in the distance. There, in the wilderness, lay the bones of countless partisans for whom a field hospital had been set up under the canopy of an enormous tree and never discovered by the German reconnaissance pilots. Their communist comrades later profaned the memory of the fallen by shooting thousands of their conquered Domobranci adversaries in the forest's crevices and sinkholes. In doing so they betrayed the cause for which they themselves had withdrawn into the forest to fight against the occupying forces in Slovenia: the dream of a free and just world. There were still a few seats free at the dark wooden tables in the taproom but when we returned from our room and tried to take our places at one of these, the hostess hustled us down a corridor to a small, bright room with four laid tables. We were the only guests and before we could look around or make any requests, we were served bowls of soup in which swam yellow and white threads of egg. Only then did we notice that the dining room was also a shrine.

Framed photographs were hung on the walls, books and manuscripts were displayed in glass cases and on the wall behind me was a panel with the facsimile of a poem and a copy of a letter from 1942. Jägerschnitzel with a side salad was already on the table; our dinner was far too rushed and the portions far too generous. Over the past few years, my appetite in the evenings had waned and for some time I'd no longer been able to polish off the servings that my wife barely touched. Still, this was not a place where it seemed wise to raise objections and certainly not to this hostess, so we had to eat up the crepes, too. Within twenty minutes, we had finished the three courses that were placed before us, unordered. At that point, we would have preferred to leave again without any fuss. But when Rina, the hostess, came to check that we'd eaten, she caught us standing before the display case. When I pointed to the photograph of an older man with round glasses, dark hair combed straight back and a determined expression on his gaunt invalid's face, she stopped her hectic bustling. 'Yes,' she replied, astonished that guests who were not from Slovenia were familiar with the name, 'that's Oton Župančič.'

This Slovenian poet had spent his childhood in this house, now hidden behind the new construction. Born near Vinica in 1878, he was sent to Ljubljana for high school. But the light that is a central to his poetry—the light of early morning and midday, nocturnal light and the light under stormy skies, the light of expectation, festive light and the light in churches—was the one he'd experienced as his element in Dragatuš. White Carniola was a poor region at the time and, like so many Gottscheers a few kilometres to the north, a great number of Slovenians left their homeland, Bela Krajina, for the

United States in search of the prosperity and freedom which the Habsburg Monarchy would never grant them. Like the two years older Ivan Cankar with whom he'd founded modern Slovenian literature and spent a few lean years in Vienna when they were young, Oton Župančič came from a family of poor petty traders. In 1892, his father had sold the house in which we were standing, as I read in the display, to the grandfather of Rina's husband whom she was now hurrying off to fetch.

Rajko Stefanić was a tall, imposing man about ten years older than I and he appeared staunchly determined to show us right then everything in the house that was related to Župančič and to tell us everything he knew about the poet. Župančič had written the 1942 letter to Rajko's father that was hanging on the wall. He was over sixty at the time and too ill to join the partisans, indeed, the photograph that showed him so clearly to be ailing was taken about that time. Yet his songs were sung among the partisans, even though Župančič wrote little that scanned or was likely to inspire men to action. The poet had brought Slovenian literature into being and in doing so had created his own role as the prophet and visionary. In small nations that are rooted in their language and survive through that language—or fail to—no matter how apolitically a visionary poet fulfils his lyrical duties, he often acquires a political significance for his nation.

We sat in the Župančič room and drank the cold red wine that Rajko poured from large vessels into half-litre pitchers and listened to what he had to tell of his grandfather and Župančič and of his father and Dragatuš. In this inconspicuous village in Bela Krajina, a village of no renown stranded in cornfields, the partisans had set up their command centre for all of Slovenia. It was betrayed in 1942 and the Luftwaffe reduced Dragatuš to rubble. I noted how varied and disastrous a part in world history had been allotted to this small village off a highway in southern Slovenia that did not even appear on my map.

Rajko, on the other hand, said that when Oton Župančič was growing up here, Dragatuš was the end of the earth. Getting to Ljubljana was an exhausting journey. Yet from the beginning, Župančič, in his puzzling existence, was bound to the wider world. He translated from no fewer than five languages into Slovenian with the confident intention of bringing world literature—Dante, Shakespeare, Goethe, Balzac, Tolstoy—to Slovenians in their own homes. Like Cankar, he suffered from the suffocating fear that history would be written without any contribution from his own nation.

We are condemned to silence in the council of nations,

watching from afar, as the new world is made.

And, like Cankar, he did not want to leave the village and people of his childhood. His most famous poem, 'Duma', is a hymn to the village and province, a great song of work in the fields and factories— and a promise that this small world was fit to take what it was missing from the greater one and to give the greater world what it had lost. It is a moving picture of a society in which progress does not march in as the great leveller.

We stood in front of the inn, for which the drinkers had left the fields a few hours earlier and in which they were now being prepared with last orders of schnaps and beer for the sad news that it would soon be closing time and they would be shown the door. A path led from here to Vinica, where one could visit the house in which the poet was born, the Oton Župančič Path across the Lahinja nature reserve. Darkness had settled like a bell jar over the village that had been so lively in the evening, and there was not a sound except for the complaints from the bar as the drunks tried to wheedle one very last round out of the adamantine hostess.

For a while we sat shivering on the balcony from which we could see nothing but the black wall before us. The cosmopolitan villager in Dragatuš who longed for glamour, nocturnal noise and trips to Vienna and Paris and who, when in those metropolises, dreamt of the peripheries had, in the darkness, become the poet of light. All of a sudden, I was presumptuously certain that I had escaped my constant fear of suffocating in small backwaters or getting lost in vast distances, right here in the wide world of Dragatuš.

The Dream of Vrzdenec: Travels with Ivan Cankar

The first of Ivan Cankar's books that I came across was his bleak novel about a teacher, *Martin Kačur: The Biography of an Idealist*, and then I read everything of his that I could get my hands on. The eponymous Martin Kačur is out of touch with the common man yet loves the idea of him; he is a person devoted to humanity who loves men as he dreams them to be, not as they are; he is, simply, an idealist who is mocked by those he believes himself an advocate for and whose life falls short in precisely those areas where he believes himself successful.

I first read this novel, set in a doomed place with the telling name Blatni Dol or 'muddy valley', thirty years ago outside of Salzburg in a small castle that was in a state of deterioration that lent it an air of enchantment for those who were simply passing by. For me, however, who had been lured by the prospect of seeing more than just the outside of the castle into taking temporary lodgings inside, the rot and mildew soon became very trying. I sat within the castle's damp walls reading the story of the schoolteacher whose boundless idealism makes him at once ridiculous and magnificent. By that time, I had decided not to make use of the teaching certificate I'd obtained a few months earlier for a career as a high-school teacher. I read the short story 'The Servant Jernej and His Justice' about the grim consequences that follow when a Slovenian servant who has been swindled out of his property 'knocks on the door of justice, not on the door of mercy', wanting only his due. When this isn't granted him in his own country, he sets off to petition the emperor in Vienna and, because he does not find justice there either, he finally takes his complaint to God. Well-supplied in my chronic fever with medications and books, I also read Cankar's *House of Mercy*, a profession of love for the young girls in a hospital who are unafraid of death because, gripped by a moribund cheerfulness, they believe that the world is ill, not they, and that only by dying will they escape this world contained entirely within Vienna's proletarian tenements.

There is more death and dying in Ivan Cankar's novellas and stories than in almost any other works of world literature. Men collapse on the side of the road, utterly exhausted by factory work; women bring three or four children into the world and go to their eternal rest by the age of thirty-five; girls waste away from consumption angelically and blossom in a final, frightening beauty, and courageous boys with artistic and rebellious natures abandon their childhood villages and find themselves in the cold-hearted big city broken, betrayed, debauched or, in the best and worst case, bought and domesticated into petty bourgeois.

Ivan Cankar who had conceived of all these dying and defeated people or, rather, whom he had copied from real life and saved in literature, lived only forty-two years; then, presumably intoxicated, he fell down a flight of stairs and died. That was on 11 December 1918 and the Austro-Hungarian monarchy, which the Slovene had bitterly and scornfully criticized, had just fallen apart.

Official Austria should be left to drown in its own shit! History teaches us that the stupidity of Austrian diplomacy has always been a great blessing for the peoples of Europe ... Now, too, it is working with great zeal to realize the Yugoslavian utopia—and with time it will perhaps actually succeed. Everything takes place according to the method of Hegelian dialectics: when stupidity reaches its climax, it becomes wisdom.

Cankar said in a 1913 speech, where he called for South Slavs to leave the Danube Monarchy and placed all his hope for the union of the Serbs, Croats and Slovenes in a common 'Yugo-Slavian' state. The speech earned him a week in prison. He would not witness how quickly the authorities in his longed-for Kingdom of Yugoslavians brought inane energy to persecuting social agitators and discontented artists like him; in just five years, the Kingdom of South Slavs shot more South Slav workers at demonstrations than were killed in Franz Joseph's prison of nations during the seventy years that followed the blood-soaked revolutions of 1848.

Cankar was the first Slovenian writer to earn his living from his writing and, accordingly, many of his letters have only one topic: money. 'More often hungry than full,' this child of lower-class parents would never work his way out of misery. Although he was honoured at thirty-five as the greatest writer of his time, throughout his life he had lived in shabby rented rooms, in the backrooms of inns and in bleak forest huts: 'Life has beaten me to a pulp, but I polished smooth rhymes.' If the concept of a national poet is a valid one, then it applies to him, the imperious and oppressed, proud and compassionate Ivan Cankar.

What exactly does 'national poet' mean? Well, that someone opened new worlds to his country's language, that he made this language with its peasant roots fit for capturing urban experiences and intellectual phenomena, that he taught it words for what is inscrutable or heretical, for decadence and uprising. Cankar broke fresh ground in so many areas that everyone invokes him or could offer good reason for invoking him: the Social Realists, the Romantics and the Symbolists, the champions of engaged literature and those proclaiming the autonomous artwork. He was lauded and reviled as a Communist, a pornographer, a religious enthusiast and a social utopian and, authentic national author that he was, each of these labels has something to it.

In 1898, Cankar left small-town Ljubljana for Vienna, where he remained for eleven unusually literarily fruitful years and the discussions between the young man from White Carniola and Oton Župančič provided the foundations for modern Slovenian literature. A significant portion of his works were written in Vienna where he lived in abject poverty in the suburban district of Ottakring, almost succumbing to the misery that surrounded him. The heroes of his Viennese tales are Czech proletarians, Slovakian seamstresses, students from the Balkans who have gone off the rails and what he displays in them with literary brilliance and social outrage is the other, pitch-black side of the splendid metropolis. They are impossibly far from that glorious, cosmopolitan city of the fin de siècle, in which wealth attained the heights of cultural refinement and lust for life was spiked with degeneracy.

When I read Cankar's Viennese sketches and stories, I felt as if I were moving through another city than the one whose wilted splendour was being praised by Hugo von Hofmannsthal or whose urbane liveliness was being mapped with great social precision by Arthur Schnitzler. The great Austrian literature of the turn of the last century, renowned throughout the world today should always be placed side by side with the literature of those Slavs who experienced Vienna as a hostile, forbidding fortress or as a moloch that devoured all their life dreams and plans. Cankar, in any case, was under no illusion with regard to the Habsburgs' Imperial and Royal state machinery (k. & k.): 'The k. & k. schools were created for the purpose of bringing up k. & k. officials, but instead they bring up mere k. & k. typewriters.'

Ivan Cankar was a rebel outraged by injustice but his literature did not exhaust itself in complaint and denunciation. A strange inner light always shines in the darkness, and his very different companion Župančič was also a poet of light. It's not the hope of political change that illuminates the darkness but a longing for beauty. I knew his work rather well before it occurred to me that there was more in it than the gloom, the morbidity of Blatni Dol, the muddy valley in which he set his fiction. In the filth and misery, in the muddy valley of his damaged life, this child of poverty, Ivan Cankar never lost his conviction that humanity hungers not only for bread and justice but also for beauty.

In a little-known sketch, first published in 1917, he found a name for this conviction: Vrzdenec. It's the name of the village not too far from Ljubljana where his mother was born: 'I have never seen Vrzdenec and it's not shown on any map. But I know for certain that it exists and is in fact quite near.' That Vrzdenec, left unmentioned by the history books, is not suitable for a national liturgy. But calling it a primitive communist collective would not do it justice either and anyone claiming to find in Vrzdenec a happily ahistorical place would certainly miss the point. 'I have never been in Vrzdenec, and I know I never will,' wrote Cankar, whose mother had said on her deathbed, 'We'll soon be in Vrzdenec,' by which she did not mean the hereafter. The utopia that he associates with his mother's vanished village is not a return to the world of yesterday with its God-fearing modesty and frugal order. In his invocation of Vrzdenec, Cankar asserted humanity's entitlement to beauty over any and every social or national demand. Beauty is neither an academic question for professors of aesthetics nor an allure subscribed to by dandies. It is nothing other than a human right, like food, housing and education and this right need not be earned by any kind of service, it devolves on each person at birth. This is what I had missed when I read Ivan Cankar's works while living in a barrack that only became a small castle again for me after I had escaped its beetle infestations, its rot and my months-long fever.

Ottakringer Straße: A Summer Walk

Ottakringer Straße leads out from the Gürtel, a multi-lane half-circle that loosely belts the city and its inner districts, 2.8 kilometres into the countryside to the hills of the Vienna Woods. It crosses Vienna's sixteenth district which was still a stretch of land with a village outside the city's gates in the middle of the nineteenth century and then in the era of accelerated industrialization it became a blue-collar suburb complete with factories and tenements within a single generation. In 1870, there were 30,000 people living in the area of Ottakring; in 1910, six times as many people lived in the city district of the same name, that is, nearly 180,000.

'The street is grey, dirty and deserted. The houses are all the same; tall, dark, silent. The eye takes it in and immediately realizes: there has never been a happy soul in this street; when Christ comes for the last time and paradise is opened, this street will be the first to return to dust.' Ivan Cankar only refers to this street in the story's title—'The Street of the Dying'—but he used Ottakringer Straße as a model. In his Vienna stories, Ottakringer Straße was not Cankar's only model for many such nameless streets in which the proletarian misery was concentrated, but it was his principal one.

'The Street of the Dying' appeared in 1908. One hundred years later, I set out one midsummer day to walk the length of Ottakringer Straße from the dying back to the living. I started where it ends, at the Ottakringer Cemetery where it was thick with the traffic of the funeral homes' black limousines. Silently, they drove up and through the gate, discretely unloaded their freight before the mortuary chapel and seldom left the cemetery grounds, it seemed to me, without completing a silent lap of honour. Wherever I looked, I saw hearses gliding majestically between the graves and the trees like death ships. The Ottakringer Straße is long, endlessly long, and yet here it peters out inconspicuously between weeds, ornamental plants and the bones of countless generations. Suddenly, it is gone. Rarely do streets after which an entire suburb is named end more unspectacularly: after a final house, Number 266 Ottakringer Straße, it is simply gone. Of course, the world does not end here. Instead, it continues as a street with a different name. However, this street soon leads out of Ottakring and out of Slovenia and no longer has much to do with Vienna or Cankar.

It was midday, and I had already been standing for a while in front of the imposing tomb of the labour leader Franz Schuhmeier which bore a statue of him in the pose of a mob orator. A legendary speaker, blessed with the verbal wit of this suburb's dialect, he had completed his education through self-study while an unskilled worker and had established the adult education school of Ottakring. Because strict ordinances against organizing were imposed on labourers at the time, he euphemistically named the first educational association 'The Apollo Smoking Club', where members did not smoke luxuriously, but instead studied and debated until smoke came from the ears of these class-conscious, education-starved labourers. As I gazed up at the face of the man on the pedestal who looked sixty-five but had only lived to the age of forty-eight, an ancient little man scurried past me, as I stood below Schuhmeier standing above. He had seen me looking up at the statue for so long and had scrutinized the statue so carefully himself as he scurried past; he seemed to want to make sure that it had not been carried off again by the enemies of the working class as it had been in February 1934. Then he announced, as if the struggle in which Schuhmeier fell had not been decided long ago, in a loud voice that did not match his shrivelled, bone-rattling body: 'They killed him too, those cowl-wearers.'

I thought that that wasn't exactly true because Schuhmeier, as far as I knew, had been shot in 1911, not by a monk but by a mentally disturbed, unemployed member of the Christian Social Party who had been repelled by the fiery speech Schuhmeier had delivered in the Imperial Council a few days earlier against 'Jesuitism, Clericalism and Superstition'. Schuhmeier's funeral turned into the largest mass demonstration held in Vienna until then. It is estimated that half a million people had walked along the Ottakringer Straße and gathered around the cemetery in the lanes along which the black limousines now glided.

Across from Schuhmeier's grave stands the monument to the victims of the hunger revolts that had erupted a few months after his murder, particularly in Ottakring. At the time, the Waldinger family lived on Ottakringer Straße, not in the rural section near the cemetery but closer to the city, near the Gürtel. They had immigrated to Vienna from Galicia and their two sons, the songwriter Ernst and the trade unionist Theo, were 15 and 7 years old at the time. Fifty years later, in exile in America where they had fled, when Austria became Ostmark, Ernst Waldinger sang praises of the proud and forever scorned workers of Ottakring who had fought so tenaciously not just for bread but also for education, and as an old man confined to his bed in his final, pain-filled years, he recalled in one of his formally strict poems the lying-in-state of the powerful plebian tribune whose corpse he had paid respects to as a teenager.

> Laid out in your coffin; your wax-pale,
> proletarian face so beloved
> and your handlebar moustache; am I not moved
> to see myself passing your corpse?
> What is it, with so many horror-filled years gone by
> that brings you, dead, before my inner eye?

And Theodore Waldinger, who did not return to Austria until his old age, but then visited for a few weeks every year, gave me a vivid account of how he had ended up in the middle of the uprising, holding his older brother's hand, as the Bosniaks rode into Ottakring on 17 September 1911, with their sables drawn to spread fear. The workers of Vienna were not massacred by soldiers from the surrounding area but by Muslim soldiers from Bosnia and Herzegovina whom no one in Vienna knew and who, wearing fezzes instead of the usual soldiers' caps, dutifully chased the workers. In the multinational state of the Habsburgs, the troops deployed to beat and shoot down demonstrators were always brought in from distant provinces of the empire. As a result, the people's hatred of the authorities turned into hatred of foreigners, a fateful heirloom from the monarchy that is still worn today and grows ever-more sordid.

The old man had gone a few metres further and was waiting at the monument of the victims of the hunger revolts as if he wanted to give me the opportunity to ask him a question. I didn't know where to start and so repeated tritely and stupidly: 'Ah, I see, the cowl-wearers!' He seemed to take my embarrassment for scorn and glared at me with his elderly eyes as forcefully as an old man's shimmering watery-blue eyes can. 'Yes, exactly,' he insisted, 'the cowl-wearers!' As we walked towards the exit together, he explained with a sad irony directed at the clueless of today like me and an unmistakable scorn directed at the authorities of yesteryear all about Austrian history and the cowl-wearer regiment. He lectured me with thoroughness and determination in an irritating tone that was at once resigned and impatient. We left the cemetery and passed a small park, which, I learnt, was named after a fire chief and when I smiled faintly at that, my companion admonished me for my inappropriate reaction as he took one unsteady step after another: 'What is amusing about the fact that the residents of Ottakring dedicated a park to their very worthy Fire Chief Karl Kantner? Conflagrations were, after all, a recurring catastrophe. In 1835, for example, fifty-two houses burned to the ground in just two hours.'

The old man showed no intention of letting me go without a convincing apology so, at the bend in the Ottakring Straße, I tried surreptitiously to lead him past the Alt-Ottakring Church, a massive building that really did have an ostentatious cowl-wearing clerical, siege-castle-like air. He probably discerned my intention because he gave me a brief, approving look when I turned my steps, and therefore his too, to the other side of the street. There were a few wine bars—in old Ottakring there had been vineyards and one legendary vintner, whose tavern we had already passed, had often said of his place, 'Men drink, horses guzzle, but here at Noibinger's, it's the reverse,' until he could no longer drag himself to the watering hole and dropped dead with a rock-hard liver. My companion's comment on this phrase, which I remembered from a book about Ottakring's local history, was that he no longer believed that drinking alcohol was irrational and that a resulting early death from drinking was justifiable.

We had been walking for more than half a kilometre and I was marvelling at the quietness of this street that still seemed rural and sedate when the old man suddenly stopped, gestured at the entrance to a five-storey building, and said that he would have to say goodbye. We shook hands and he looked me in the eye once more and said in the tone of someone sending a schoolboy out alone into the wide world: 'You're not a stupid man. Still, beware of prevailing opinions!' He hadn't told me his name or answered my question as to his profession and now I wondered if he was the Joseph Svitak or the Dr Kappel whose names could still be deciphered on the doorbell panel.

I headed towards the beginning of Ottakringer Straße intent on being wary of prevailing opinions and increasingly ill-humoured because it still bore no resemblance to the street I had read and heard so much about for years, a street that is, where the old Viennese who had been newcomers just two generations earlier had become the fearful or angry minority pushed aside by the newcomers. No matter how hard I tried to find some of the splendour or misery of a multicultural street, there was no trace, nothing thrilling or ghastly. What stood out about the street was its ordinariness with its alternating colourful and faded grey facades, its shops, kindergartens, apartment buildings, coffeehouses, its loud but not hellish traffic, and all the people who were nothing other than villagers you find in other big cities.

Two men in their forties were sitting in Café Ritter, one of them sallow with lank, bleached hair, the other puffy with a bright-red complexion, and both seemed rather battered by life. They were caught up in a discussion in the local dialect that was curious, not because they were both slurring their speech slightly but because each answered the other only after a long pause for thought:

'Know what, you're just not using all your potential.'

'What potential would that be?'

'Are you saying you're not a man?'

'If you like.'

Heimito von Doderer called the Ottakring dialect the 'primeval swamp of language par excellence' and not at all condescendingly but rather in recognition of the fact that in Ottakring the Viennese dialect could be found in a productive, primal state out of which it repeatedly creates itself anew.

Having walked briskly after leaving the cafe, I was closer to the beginning of Ottakringer Straße than its end and I noticed a side street that forked off to right. The Lindauergasse, I had learnt from Ivan Cankar's books, was once an alley of the consumptive, the dying and the dead who were destined to remain among the half-dead for a few more days or years. This side street had no charm today either, with its municipal residential buildings built in the 1960s lacking any aesthetic considerations or intentions and a shabby-looking three-storey house with a small plaque indicating that the Slovenian writer Ivan Cankar had lived there from 1899.

This building at Number 26, now painted yellow, was no longer the drab tenement where Cankar had rented a tiny room in the cramped, stuffy apartment of the large Löffler family. Mrs Löffler slaved away all day long to feed her family and the girls rose early, too, to contribute to the family's meagre living with hours of sewing. In numerous vignettes and articles, Cankar captured the atmosphere of their lives, imbued with hunger and the longing for a better life, constriction and generosity. The youngest daughter, Amalia, died of consumption and in his novel *The Ward of Our Lady of Mercy*. Cankar, who had often visited Amalia in hospital in her final weeks, created a memorial for her and the other emaciated girls, eyes glowing with fever, who crept through the city.

The oldest daughter, Steffi, became his lover. She was the model of countless girls and women in his socially critical novellas and stories. She remained his eternal fiancée since the foreign future groom delayed the wedding year after year because he was busy working in a tiny room on what today are considered classic works of modern Slovenian literature, because he didn't have enough money to start his own household and because he still intended to sort out this or that before . . . In 1909, he moved back to Ljubljana from Ottakring—'where the houses were gloomy and the streets bleak' and 'everyone had gaunt faces and patched clothing'. For a time, he continued to write Steffi, already too old to find a husband, by the standards of the time, letters filled with complaints about the misery of trying to be a Slovenian writer in Ljubljana, but with very few words about the misery she was suffering, abandoned in Vienna by her Slovenian writer-lover. The letters gradually became less frequent and finally stopped altogether.

Although he had lived in Vienna for ten years, Cankar had met almost exclusively with other Slovenes and other Slavic nationals aside from the proletarians and lumpen in his neighbourhood. He never met the era's great Viennese writers, like Schnitzler or Hofmannsthal, and apparently hardly any poets of the working class, reporters covering the lower classes or editors at the socialist newspapers. Just as in Prague at the turn of the last century or in the now excessively mythologized Trieste, writers in Vienna were strictly divided by nationality with few connections between the groups. They had their own cafes, newspapers and meeting rooms. Cankar lived in Vienna for a decade and wrote a work of world literature but didn't know a single Viennese author or publisher, only seamstresses, industrial workers, day labourers, maids—and Slovenes, Slovenian poets and doctors, students and workers.

Back on Ottakringer Straße, I noticed for the first time the many laundrettes you find in cities all over the world where young people who don't want to stay in the area long enough to make buying a washing machine worthwhile as well as many men who have left their families to earn money abroad live alone. And between the laundrettes, tailors offering their services, recalling a time when broken things were still repaired rather than simply thrown away and worn spots on clothing were still patched or mended and suits were hemmed and taken in for younger siblings.

This atmosphere seemed to belong so much to a world of yesteryear, I almost forgot that I was making my way through the Vienna of tomorrow. I was reminded of this by the shop window of the 'Partizan Butik', a shop selling memorabilia of the football club Partizan Belgrade which had won great international success in an earlier era and produced some of the best players of Yugoslavia. Today it is notorious for its fan base. They have associations in many cities around the world and in Austria, their headquarters are at Ottakringer Straße 65. True to the reputation the football club had to defend, the shop gave the impression that you could get equipped more easily for the next civil war than find a woollen scarf in the team's black-and-white colours. Partizan fans call themselves 'Grobari' or 'gravediggers' and enjoy a singular reputation not only as thugs among hooligans all over Europe but especially as pyrotechnicians always setting off fireworks in sold-out stadiums and spreading waves of panic.

After I'd looked at the many things necessary to be a football fan fit for military service, I left the shop accompanied by the young salesman. His hair was cropped short in a military cut, although his figure was hardly athletic or soldierlike, tending instead to a well-nourished roundness. He stepped out onto Ottakringer Straße armed only with a broom and headed for one of the piles the Viennese favourite animals are sure to leave behind on the pavement and which a four-legged inhabitant of the asphalt jungle had deposited right in front of the Butik's shop window. The salesman shook his head as if he could hardly fathom such uncivilized behaviour and set about cleaning the pavement in front of his shop. When I said goodbye, he said something in Ottakringer dialect that convinced me of von Doderer's theory of linguistic creation: '*Stette überalla, dass fiar die Hunta musstu Sackal nemma, aba nix di Wiena tutta.*' (It's posted everywhere that you've got to bring a waste bag for your dog, but none of the Viennese do.)

Traffic grew thicker and louder closer to the Gürtel, especially since, although fewer cars drove here, most of their drivers liked to stop on the street or on the pavement and take a break outdoors, talking with friends and relatives with the motor running. This was it then, the 'Balkan mile' as journalists dubbed it, with rows of Turkish and Serbian snack bars, stores and bars with proto-Balkan names like 'Balkan Best Club'. To the right, Yppengasse led to Yppenplatz, a modestly sized square set over an old air-raid shelter with the stands of several elegant market shops in the centre and many cafes and taverns along the edges. Tables and chairs had been set out, and several hundred people were sitting outside enjoying the summery afternoon; it wasn't exactly a festival of international fraternization since the Austrians seemed to be sitting apart from the Turks, the Serbs, each group separate and distinct but still in the harmonious atmosphere of a lively village in the middle of a big city.

'The street is grey, dirty and deserted,' Ivan Cankar had written 100 years earlier, but life here was colourful and richly diverse. That there'd never been a happy soul here, as Cankar claimed, was a message from a time long past because it was clear that most of those gathered here had not been driven onto the street by their unhappiness but had come for the joy of this street and this place, the joy of the city. What were the prevailing opinions I was meant to be wary of? This was neither the slum whose residents were being demonized by some, nor the idyll that others were propagandizing—this was just the city alive with its many voices and images.

CHAPTER FOUR

On Making an Appearance in Siena

It was my third day in Siena, and I was sitting outside, changing cafes periodically to face now this side, now that side of the famous piazza that slopes down from the edges towards the centre with a contour often compared to a clamshell. From the lack of rain, despite weeks of overcast skies, the facades of the buildings and palazzi were so desiccated that their Tuscan elegance had an air of desert sands. Wherever I drank an iced tea or one of my far-too-many espressos, the bill was set down with the glass or cup and the server waited persistently for immediate payment, standing next to me and gazing in boredom at the Piazza del Campo. There weren't many tourists in the city yet, and on the cafe terraces I was surrounded by locals, loud retirees who gestured emphatically and seemed to be caught up in a passionate argument at every hour of the day, whether about tomorrow's football match or yesterday's pasta. Immediate payment was demanded not only of tourists but also of Italians, even the regulars. This precautionary measure was unpleasantly businesslike, but it was not directed at foreigners—although the waiters may well have recognized me as one. They didn't suspect each person of possibly being a dangerous foreigner as we did but of being a cheat who could very well be one of their own.

I had come to this city famous for its beauty to present the translation of a work of reportage I had written about the Roma in a village that was sinking into the mire, a book about the hatred incurred by the residents of the slum and about the indifference with which they bore it all—the mire, the hatred—themselves. I stayed for two days after the presentation because I knew Siena from a visit thirty years earlier and I was hoping, after so much time had passed, to encounter myself in the streets and alleys. Myself, that is the person I was thirty years ago, including the person I did not become. The past 'I' is always greater and richer that the present one who has evolved through a constant process of rejection, surrender, renunciation, escape, a diminishing of the many possibilities contained in him, just as the 'I' of tomorrow will arise from the waning of today's.

The beggarwoman I had noticed on my first evening began her day's work at ten in the morning and she stayed on the Campo, which she constantly circled or crossed and recrossed, until ten at night when she would disappear into one of the alleys and head for home. The enormous clamshell was her territory. In a shabby, colourful cloak, she slowly walked to and fro between the Palazzo Pubblico and the fountain or in a circle past the fancy shops, guest houses and cafes. She was a Roma, probably from Slovakia, and as she trudged along with her open hand outstretched, constantly pleading even with those most hostile to her, not letting herself be turned away but pestering people insistently until they were willing to buy her off with a few coins, she completely corresponded in the way she went about her work to the image that respectable citizens of beautiful cities had of the shameless Roma beggars of Eastern Europe.

She was probably not over forty, although her angular face with its sandy, weather-beaten complexion made her look older, and she had long ago given up what only the completely lost have to lose, that is any interest in her own appearance and behaviour. One might well have believed that what she schlepped across the Campo all day long was not her body but her work-tool, the only thing she had and an implement she herself had become. When I left a cafe to wander around the old city in search of myself, our paths would cross and when I returned and looked for a seat along the edge of the piazza, our paths crossed again. Yet she never begged from me of all people—who was in Siena because I'd written a book about the Roma of Svinia and had long had a euro coin ready for her in my trouser pocket—as if she didn't believe I would give her anything.

On one of my walks, I entered a narrow street and after a few metres found myself before an unassuming synagogue. I couldn't remember having passed this way before, although that surely was the case since, after all, I had spent an entire week walking around Siena on my last visit and had much more stamina as a city walker then than today. A plaque informed me that in 1799, thirteen Jews suspected of being involved with the godless Jacobins and the French Revolution were chased to the nearby Campo and hanged there by the Legionnaires of Mary. Not far from the synagogue, I came upon a small, modestly equipped playground where no children were playing. Instead, four adults sat on the backrest of a wooden bench, smoking in silence and occasionally spitting on the gravel. I sat on the far side of the playground, on a bench on the other side of the sandbox and the rusty slide and leafed diligently through the travel guide that I carried with me only to have something at hand in such situations.

The four men may have already been killing time for hours with their silence, smoking and spitting; they'd learnt the art of waiting better than I, with my constant need to be doing something, even if just pretending to read a book. When I looked up, they followed my glance with interest as if they might discover something in a far corner of the playground that had eluded them until then. When our eyes met, they gave friendly, embarrassed grins and when I stood up, they slipped off the backrest of their bench. They didn't want any money from me, just a bit of distraction since they had to spend their days waiting and not begging like their wives, and when I passed them, they smiled so sadly and humbly in their destiny of boredom that I wondered who bore the more difficult share: the women who had to earn sustenance by begging from people who disdained them or these men who had reduced their existence solely to bearing time, to waiting for morning to eventually become noon and, after each midday, for night to come.

They were from Prešov, I learnt, a city I had once stopped in while researching my reportage. Slovakia is a country with many lovely small towns that have not yet been discovered by European tourists and I remembered Prešov as the loveliest of them all. The elongated, spindle-shaped main square with a Gothic Catholic church in its centre and, almost leaning against it, the Protestants' Renaissance church, is to the Slovakians what Siena's Piazza del Campo is to the Italians: an exceptional artwork generously placed in the city, a public ceremonial space for the residents, the heart of urban life and city culture . . . The events held on both squares included not only festivities but also executions (which the authorities sometimes presented as festivities to the public who needed to be entertained). The First World War ended a few months late in Prešov because during the transition from the last days of war to the first days of peace, scattered soldiers of the Imperial and Royal Army proclaimed their own city state before finally being vanquished and forty-one of them dangled from the streetlamps at the marketplace.

Not far this spot, I happened on a synagogue that was much more magnificent than the one in Siena and the old man guiding me through it said that the mood at the time demanded a pogrom but in this case the victims were not the few Jews left in Prešov. The lovely city actually did make international headlines a few months after my visit because the town council had given in to the residents' demand and built a 2-metre-high wall around a run-down neighbourhood. The justification for building this wall—fifteen years after the large one that cut through Europe had fallen—was that the industrious and upright citizens could no longer be expected to constantly have to look at the misery into which the Roma's quarter had sunk.

Evenings were chilly at the Campo and people sat in front of the restaurants under mobile heaters that shot out of the ground like glowing mushrooms. I ate outside at a restaurant over which the Palazzo Sansedoni towered, looking over at the city hall and the still-not-illuminated Torre del Mangia. I was surprised that so little light from the time I spent in Siena, thirty years ago, shone on my current way through the city today and that the sights were familiar to me from countless pictures and illustrations in books, but I had no memory of what I had once seen and experienced here. I recognized buildings and squares, followed the right direction almost instinctively to reach a particular square but I didn't see myself, didn't see the one who had walked and spent time here and even the Hotel La Perla on the Piazza dell'Independenza, where I had spent a week in a cheap room on the second floor, failed to tell me any stories when I unexpectedly found myself standing in front of it.

The beggarwoman had quit. Of course, where misery cannot be eliminated, the wretched must become invisible—that was the point of the wall. In the darkness, a seventy-year-old man in a tracksuit was running laps in the square where twice a year horses gallop. He ran with buckling knees that seemed barely able to support the weight of his skinny body and several tables cheered him on when he shuffled more than ran past for the sixth or seventh time. The air was cold but the wine glass in my hand was warm. I looked out over the square that many claim is the most beautiful in Italy and that the Frommer's guidebook rapturously claimed was an antechamber of paradise and I was glad that the Roma have emerged from the limbo in which they were meant to stay hidden and make their appearance all over Europe. Their physical presence is the only chance we have to remember them—the invisible ones.

Piccolomini (The Neo-Latinists I)

He was born in Corsignano, a small town not far from Siena, but spent twenty-three years of his life north of the Alps. His paths took him through half of Europe and wherever he went, he left something behind: a son in Scotland, for example, in Basel, the most important documents from the Council that met for many years, and in Austria, it was Chancery humanism—a concept that sounds paradoxical to us today—with which the state took the decisive step from the Middle Ages into the modern era. This widely travelled man's favourite city was Vienna, although his descriptions of the city in his letters are equal parts disapproving and charmed.

His letters, notably, were sent all over Europe, not only because he wrote to his students scattered throughout princely courts in Germany, France, Sweden, Bohemia and Poland, who formed the first shock troops of Italian humanism, but also because each of his letters in this last era before the invention of the printing press was copied many times and circulated within Europe's nascent scholarly world. These letters exerted a strong stylistic influence on an entire age and were taken as the model of how to construct a letter formally and rhetorically, quite aside from the enormous impact of the requests, demands, reprimands and condemnations they contained. In his letters from Vienna, he wrote, half-amazed, half-horrified, of the 'unbelievable amount of wine' the Viennese shipped into the city from their country houses and vineyards and noted that every third building was a wine tavern. Indeed 'the entire population attaches great importance to food and drink. Whatever they've earned through the week is gulped down before the start of the next.'

Aeneas Silvio Piccolomini, whose parents were not particularly well-off, was too much of a bon vivant not to see the appeal of this lifestyle and too much of a rationalist championing the sound development of a reasonable state not to see its dangers. No city has a greater number of prostitutes, he wrote, less outraged than astonished because in Vienna it was in any case customary even for decently married women not to refuse the advances of men who were themselves decently married, giving rise to a brisk level of social intercourse. What this man, who took his intellectual measure from antiquity and was probably the first to develop from ancient thought something like a framework for Europe and a kind of European self-image and self-awareness, liked most about Vienna was the ceaseless movement that seemed to reign over this city of foreigners and new-comers who rapidly became fervent and respected Viennese, this city in which recently settled merchants married in advanced age their young maids and, with welcome speed, made them affluent widows who then married their previous lovers, such that domestic servants were elevated to the class of rich merchant within less than one generation.

All this deeply fascinated Aeneas Silvio Piccolomini because, as the most influential adviser of the Habsburg emperor Frederick III, himself a man of order, he knew all too well that the old order of the Middle Ages had to be pried loose and crumble in order to create an opening for what he considered progress although it wasn't called such at the time. His idea of progress was a state with a single, learned ruler who was not surrounded with a bored aristocracy but with a class of educated men who could give him knowledgeable advice about everything he didn't know—and with a common, educated tongue in which scholars, diplomats, chancellors and chancery clerks in all of Europe could communicate: Neo-Latin.

As a poet, Aeneas Silvio Piccolomini immortalized his experiences in erotic matters in suggestive verses which was possible for him to do because Italian humanism, through which he had rediscovered antiquity, also advanced the idea that each person is a separate entity, an individual who is not standardized but able to have personal experiences and is entitled to them. The novella, *Euralius and Lucretia*, a tragic love story in which the male protagonist is unmistakably modelled on the Habsburg chancellor Kaspar Schlick and the female on a renowned Sienese beauty, went through thirty-five editions in the fifteenth century alone—and influenced erotic narratives for two or three centuries. Piccolomini was almost forty when he wrote it in 1444. Two years later, he had been so richly rewarded in the service of Pope Eugen IV that for want of wealth the pope had to resort to rewarding him with religious titles. And so, at the age of forty-one, this father of several children, author of erotic novellas and poems, courtier and bon vivant reluctantly allowed himself to be ordained a priest and the very next year was named Bishop of Trieste and then Bishop of Siena—ten years later, he was elected pope.

I stood before the Libreria Piccolomini in Siena Cathedral. From the outside this exorbitant church building, extolled by art historians as an important cathedral, did not make a compelling impression on me but, rather, an expressly uncomfortable one; yes, the flamboyant facade with its three portals and myriad statues does evoke the 'wedding cake' Julien Green saw in it and found downright hideous. In the nave at the time there were maybe thirty visitors, gathered in groups of three to five, discussing the opulence of the cathedral interior which was much less ostentatious and evident in the elegant black-and-white marble, an opulence that has a more powerful effect on the observer than does the facade's overpowering excess.

In the left side aisle, I saw an enormous marble facade with capitals, pilaster strips, two arches, a whole assortment of eagles, raptors, crescent moons, sea horses and the Piccolomini family crest. The Libreria was commissioned thirty years after the death of Aeneas Silvio, whose papal name was Pius II, by his nephew to serve a purpose it never would fulfil, namely, to collect and preserve his uncle's legendary library. When I stepped from the darkness of the massive portal into the library, the latter was bathed in an almost unearthly light which fell from two large windows opposite the entrance. As monumental as the Libreria appeared, it was much too small to fit all the books, folios, letters and cosmographies Piccolomini had collected—some of which he had written himself. So there I was in a library almost devoid of books because only the cathedral's ancient and very impressive hymn books were displayed on the chest-high row of wooden bookshelves that wrapped around the room. Every inch of the walls, in contrast, was covered with glowing frescoes illustrating scenes from the pope's life from the scholarly young man setting off to the Council of Basel, which he, a layperson, attended as the Bishop of Fermo's secretary, to his speech before James I of

Scotland, his coronation as imperial poet in the court of Frederick III, to his arrival, infirm and mortally ill, in Ancona. He had set out for Ancona in 1464 intending to lead the united European armies against Constantinople.

Aeneas Silvio Piccolomini was an aesthete and free spirit, a virtuoso of the word who prided himself on his ability to write love poems that were indistinguishable from those of the most risqué Classical poets, Propertius and Ovid, who wrote books on Bohemia and Emperor Frederick III, and who—as the only pope before the Polish one who followed more than 500 years later—wrote his autobiography and completed at least two volumes (*De Europa* and *De Asia*) of his cosmography. Yet this scholar had only one goal once he became pope: the crusade against Constantinople. It is illuminating to see how this man, perhaps the first scholar of the Renaissance to have an image of Europe as a whole, not one limited to the splendid and powerful cities or states, how this man who had disciples in Prague, Krakow and Pécs, spoke of Dalmatia, Wallachia and Croatia as European countries and did not forget to include the Transylvanian Saxons and the Rascians as the Serbs were long called in his great invocation of Europe. It is, indeed, illuminating to see how he, the first one to frame Europe as a realistic vision in the early modern period, envisioned an anti-Europe at the same time.

Europe has only ever been able to conceive of itself in contrast to an anti-Europe, to a realm of barbarism, of impiety, of regression, against which it posited itself as a realm of civilization, religious faith or progress. Europe has no awareness of itself without that entity branded as anti-Europe. And so Pope Pius II, humanist that he was, lived for the war he wanted to wage against the Ottomans. Admittedly, one must assert against the void of memory, he did not champion war against the heathens or call for the death of the infidels or

71

plan the conquest of Jerusalem. He had one goal: the Byzantine Empire, Constantinople, the metropolis of Christendom in south-eastern Europe, which was holy to him not only because it was the Christian metropolis of the east but also because it represented a connection to the ancient world and thus bound two things that are discussed again today: Classical antiquity and Christendom.

To Pius II, Constantinople was nothing other than the internal western cohesion that united the Classical heritage and Christianity. But Constantinople fell to the Ottomans in 1453 and was incorporated into their rapidly expanding empire. He was not driven by the same raging religious zeal to lay pious waste to the pagans that sent medieval crusaders to Jerusalem and compelled them to set fire to Jewish communities on their way. Pius II had spoken out unusually vehemently for his time against slavery and the persecution of the Jews. What drove him was not the old crusaders' longing to free the holy city by drowning others and themselves in blood. Instead, it was the hope of reconquering the bridge between Classical antiquity and Christendom. This reconquest would not have been a peaceful endeavour without bloodshed; indeed, ten years earlier Constantinople had not fallen to the Ottomans peacefully and without bloodshed.

Aeneas Silvio Piccolomini died in Ancona before his military expedition could begin and after his death it was not undertaken. On the last fresco that shows him in the Libreria Piccolomini, he is depicted as an ashen old man on a palanquin gazing down sideways at the ground with a strangely absent expression as if he had long been aware of the futility of what he longed to fight for.

CHAPTER FIVE

The Dead Woman of Sélestat

One can die anywhere, but I never expected that Sélestat, of all places, a tidy little town that seemed to have been lost in a Sunday afternoon torpor for decades, would take on such an unseemly significance for me and this made me feel a bit indignant. The pressure in my chest had grown ever-stronger since breakfast and by the time we parked the car on the Quai des Pêcheurs, a street that looked conspicuously shabby in this neat town, my shirt was sticking, wet, to my back. I felt dizzy: it was that internal dizziness in which you can walk a perfectly straight line, yet still fear some kind of internal collapse so that your legs, which can keep moving for hours, carry nothing but an empty shell. We passed a small amusement park with only one carousel, on which a handful of children circled on brown plastic horses or in colourful space capsules, watched by their pale mothers, themselves nearly minors, standing close together, exhausted, smoking and mechanically raising a hand to wave at their children as they orbited past again. I would have liked to join them: 'Mesdames, some time ago, a time which fled so rapidly, I, too, waved at my children as they passed on the carousel and when I consider it now, on this afternoon with my heart about to break— it was the best time of my life, when our children were still little and we had so much to do that we sometimes woke up in the morning already exhausted.'

We continued on our way, without my confiding in the mothers of Sélestat or offering them words of encouragement, into the section of streets, alleys and squares that make up the small historic centre of Sélestat, a city that could not have always been as insignificant as it was now—that said, the place where one dies is never completely insignificant, at least not for oneself. We walked around two churches that rose from the tangle of alleys with a massiveness we had not expected and, afraid that my difficulty breathing could possibly bring an embarrassing end to my valiant life as an atheist by making me sink to my knees and raise my eyes beseechingly to the crucifix, I did not enter either one but waited outside while my wife visited them. She came out of the Sainte-Foy Church remarking that it had a beautiful Romanesque interior not too spoiled by Baroque decorations of later generations, then looked at me with concern and declared: 'What a sight you are!'

We found a bistro that was still open. Inside, only one table was occupied by three elderly men conversing in a strange language, perhaps the renowned Alsatian dialect, of which I understood not a single word and which, in fact, spoken as quickly and with such peculiar hissing as these men, hardly recalled the sound of German at all, even though Elsässerditsch is a very old dialect of it. Sélestat was once called Schlettstadt and in the Middle Ages was a Free Imperial City. It was then, like all of Alsace, caught up in the centuries-long battles between France and Germany that visited so much devastation on the region and made it difficult for the inhabitants to remain what they were: people of a borderland who shared equally in German and French culture and for whom having to opt for one or the other always entailed a loss and betrayal—loss and betrayal, even for the many who, carried away by nationalistic propaganda and seduced by the small advantages promised by the victorious side of the moment, suddenly wanted to be the best French citizens or the staunchest Germans.

In the First World War, many Alsatians fought on the German side, others with the French army and in 1918, when Alsace fell once again to France, it was advisable for all of them to proudly profess their allegiance to the French fatherland, just as in 1939, when the National Socialists incorporated Alsace into the Gau Oberrhein, they had to declare themselves true Germans, steeled in the Volkstum battles of the borderlands. At the same time, they hardly had grounds to be proud of the *Grande Nation* that would only accept them if they renounced their native language, as was required of the Corsicans, the Occitan or the Bretons, and they had no reason to consider themselves forward posts of Germanness, not least because most of them did not speak High German but Alsatian, which was not suitable for communication with Germans of the Reich, as it was a regional language in which the particular history of their land had become word and sound.

Each of the three elderly men had a small glass of red wine from which he would take a sip every few minutes while clasping it in a firm grip the entire time. The waitress was young and could not speak any German, nor Alsatian, so she talked to the old men and to us in French. She brought me a cup of chamomile tea, a drink I had always loathed, and only drank now out of the conviction that God or the Fates would surely reward my willingness to choke this liquid down with a spontaneous healing of any disease whatsoever. I listened to the old men who knew how to drink sedately and still debate so passionately and I was reminded of another old man who had died in Chicago, fifteen years ago, whose voice I still had in my ear, a man who had managed to preserve his pronounced Kakanian-inflected Viennese dialect over the fifty years he had lived in the United States after being forced to flee his homeland. Theo Waldinger, already an old man when we became friends, had sat at our large kitchen table and, in passing, told me, infected as I was by his characteristic curiosity, that he planned on going to Colmar the following week because he wanted, before the black Orcus devoured him—those were his words—to stand before the Isenheim Altarpiece which he knew from many reproductions and books on art history but had never seen with his own eyes.

Colmar is not far from Sélestat and we had initially planned to drive directly to that celebrated and far more splendid city. The only reason we were not already in Colmar had to do with Sélestat itself —the existence of which we had still been unaware that very morning—and with my growing unease, which led us to take a random exit off the highway so I could get out of the car and walk, something that had often helped me regain a measure of calm and confidence. To the sound of the three elderly men arguing tirelessly and the sound of Theo Waldinger's voice in my head, I looked around the long, narrow bistro furnished with the industrial clutter of placelessness and I brooded over what little I knew of the peculiar Elsässerditsch language. Then I heard my wife's voice as she remarked, impressed, that I had actually dozed off over a cup of chamomile tea in a French bistro at four in the afternoon.

Outside it had grown even cooler, the amusement park was deserted; the carousel stood still, the tired mothers had taken their children home. We encountered only one small group of tourists not far from the St Georges Church standing near a building that looked like one of those old stone market halls and bore the curved inscription 'Stadtbibliothek—Museum' on the top of its facade with the horizontal inscription 'Bibliothèque Humaniste' underneath. A sign said the museum was closed that day, but just as we approached the small group of travellers, the portal was opened from inside and a young man, who looked exactly as one would picture a seminarian with a wispy moustache on his rosy face, waved us in with an air of shy friendliness. This city's library, whose name I had first become aware of a short while before, houses an incomparable collection of manuscripts and incunabula, particularly writings and books of the early humanists, bequeathed by Beatus Rhenanus to his native city of Schlettstadt where he died in 1547 after a long intellectual peregrination. Philosophers, historians and theologians still come from all over the world in order to study the manuscripts and letters left by Beatus Rhenanus, we were told by the young man who had not overcome his shyness but still seemed happy to lead us through the library. Similarly, bibliophiles from many countries seek out the library because no other collection boasts such memorable masterpieces from the infancy of printing, an art which had one of its cradles in Alsace, as is well known.

I was always susceptible to the thrill that takes hold at the sight of long rows of folios in old libraries and yet I felt drawn back to the museum's entrance hall. There stood the bust of a young woman imbued with an aura of mysterious, even enraptured gravity. I was astonished, even a shade appalled, to learn that it was not a work of art but the head of a woman who had died almost 1,000 years ago, probably of the plague, according to the sign. Her corpse had been cast in lime to prevent contagion and so was found almost completely undamaged during building renovations. With her severe but at the same time vulnerable beauty, the dead woman from

1,000 years ago was a heartrending sight from which I could barely tear myself away though I believed it one that should be forbidden to me and everyone else. As I gazed at her, my guilty conscience towards the dead woman inspired the fleeting thought that were I to collapse outside in an alley of Sélestat, they might cast me in lime, too, and pitilessly display me to posterity. I am convinced it was the dead woman from Sélestat with her unearthly gravity and her earthly defencelessness who saved my life that afternoon; for my indignation at the sight of a human being whose eyes have been extinguished, who can no longer see a thing, being put so completely at the mercy of posterity's shameless staring—a human being therefore unable even in death to obtain the only prerogative of the dead, that is, to disappear from the face of the earth, this indignation revived me.

The next day we drove past Colmar where we had intended to stay a day or two, freed from the oppressive pressure that had led me the day prior to discover the town of Sélestat and to marvel at and feel regret for the dead woman of Sélestat. I said to myself almost cheerfully that we still had time enough to return one day and stand before the Isenheim Altarpiece before the black Orcus devoured us, too. 'The dead woman saved me,' I said to my wife who was bravely steering the car through Alsace. 'Which dead woman?' 'The one in the Bibliothèque Humaniste, of course!' 'Ah yes, that one, a beautiful work.' 'What do you mean, a work?' We started to argue and decided to postpone our argument until that afternoon when we would have time in Mulhouse to leaf through the materials we had brought with us from Sélestat and determine which of us was right. What we gathered from the brochure was that the dead woman's head in the library was what is called a natural cast and that the dead woman, who was probably Emperor Frederick Barbarossa's great-grandmother, afforded us the only natural view of a person from the early Middle Ages precisely because her features were not produced by a sculptor but rendered from her own face by a craftsman.

In my distress and outrage, I had been misled and to this misconstrual I owed my survival. It was, nevertheless, death's mistake that saved my life.

Beatus Rhenanus (The Neo-Latinists II)

The Bibliothèque Humaniste of Sélestat's holdings include a collection of Beatus Rhenanus' correspondence with men like Erasmus of Rotterdam, Johannes Reuchlin and many other great reformers of his time. Like the Italian, Dutch, German and French humanists, this Alsatian wrote his letters and studies in Neo-Latin rather than his mother tongue. (But were the mother tongues of students in monastery schools and other religious institutions really Alsatian or Flemish, Provençal or Tuscan, or not—since these young men saw their biological mothers so rarely—rather Latin, the language of the Holy Mother Church?) The fact that, long after they'd left monastery life behind, the former students continued not only to write in Neo-Latin but to do so in styles that were astonishingly supple, sensual, voluptuous and rich in poetic imagery is inseparable from their great discovery of Classical Antiquity, which they, the proponents of humanism and the Renaissance, opposed to a medieval age whose image had darkened within a few generations. Yet the decision to write in Neo-Latin is even more closely connected to the readership these learned men had in mind, a readership that, in the era before Europe had invented its nations, was a European republic of scholars.

Fittingly, Beatus Rhenanus, too, had written a history of the Germans—not in German but in Neo-Latin, under the title *Rerum Germanicum libri tres*. What is so distinctive about this work and the reason people still travel to Sélestat today to study it in the very place it was written are Beatus Rhenanus' reliable critical readings of his source texts. These allow us to observe an early philosopher of the Enlightenment as he creates his own tools of anti-dogmatism. The critique of the Western world's historical and religious origins is one the Christian religion needed to combine with reason to the extent possible for a religion that must not surrender the numinous as its core, a critique that, after a long struggle, finally constrained the Church within secular bounds. This critique, moreover, was developed in the very bosom of the Church and was first practiced in the secret language of the ordained and the adept.

My topic is the sixteenth century but I am speaking of the present, of Europe, and of myself: of Europe which is in the process of forgetting how it originated; of myself as someone who often meets upstanding people convinced that Europe would have come to its senses much earlier if only it had known how to free itself from the yoke of religion sooner. It is a strange world, indeed, when it falls to the non-believers to remember the importance of Christianity for the Enlightenment.

Apropos: Janus Pannonius (The Neo-Latinists III)

In the middle of the fifteenth century in Dalmatia, there was a young man who grew up to become an Italian scholar, a Croatian humanist, a Hungarian bishop, an Austrian writer and an outlaw refugee. In the few Austro-Hungarian history books in which he has earned a footnote, he is called Janus Cecinge; in the few works of Balkan literary history that dedicate a few pages to the early period before the invention of a national standard written language, he is instead referred to as Ivan Česmički. The name he gave himself, however, is Janus Pannonius. Because Dalmatia was under Venetian rule at the time, he was educated in Italy in the legendary court of Leonello d'Este in Ferrara under the mentorship of the learned Guarino da Verona who had established humanism in Ferrara. Guarino praised the sixteen-year-old: 'when he spoke Latin, he seemed to have been born in Rome; when he spoke Greek, he seemed to have been born in Athens.' But this Croatian, educated to be an Italian humanist in Ferrara and appointed Archbishop of Pécs (or Fünfkirchen) by the Hungarian King Matthias Corvinus who wanted to introduce the accomplishments of Western humanism into his chancelleries—this child of four peoples continued to write in Latin.

Threatened by intrigues and having fallen into disfavour through unfortunate political vicissitudes, he was forced to flee to a Croatian village, where he died at thirty-eight, in a damp priory, but not before he had composed his own epitaph: 'Here lies Janus, the first to have brought the laurel-wreathed Muses from Helicon's heights to the banks of his native Ister.' This beautifully illustrates the contradiction—unfortunately no longer decipherable for us today—that ran even more painfully through the classically educated humanists of the Balkans than through their brothers-in-spirit in the West, with whom they maintained lively communication. In the Latin inscription, which Pannonius composed himself, he calls on Helicon, the Greek home of the Muses in order to give himself credit, as heir of the crowned singers of antiquity, for having made the Muses a home on the banks of the Ister, the ancient name for the Danube.

Before nations were invented, dialects normalized as national languages and poetry appointed the guardian of national consciousness, there was a longing to implant and cultivate a European culture on the same level as that of ancient Greece throughout the region. For want of nations that could rise from the jumble of regional tribes and empower themselves as such and for want of codified languages with which nations would later identify themselves, this longing could only express itself in a language understood by the learned across the breadth of Europe and not by those who lived along the Rhine, the Vistula or the Danube, in the Vosges, the Dolomites or the Carpathian Mountains. It was an Enlightenment without a people, succeeded by the national mobilization without intellect.

CHAPTER SIX

The Rain of Brno:
Ivan Blatný and the Moravian Portuguese Poet

You must go to Brno to see the rain. There are writers who have written almost exclusively about Brno and almost exclusively about what it's like there when it rains. Brno in the rain is a sadder place than anywhere else in the world, but in a less personally inflected way: the Brno rain washes sadness clean of all private elements, of all despondency and dejection, until it is nothing but immaculate, essential sadness.

Just as we stepped into the great Freedom Square, Náměstí Svobody, which frankly cannot be called beautiful, although it does have a certain charm that transcends the beauty of a few of its individual edifices, it started raining—right on schedule. We had just had three days of continuously sunny weather travelling through Moravia, yet we hadn't doubted for a minute that we would reach Brno in the rain.

Wider on the north end and narrowing towards the south, the almost-triangular Freedom Square, intersected along its length by tram tracks, immediately began to glisten with moisture, and not just the asphalt, which seemed to me fashioned especially to gleam in wet conditions, but also the palace of the industrialist Klein, the Renaissance palace of the wine merchant Schwarz, the slender plague column of the Catholic Church, which had set in Brno one of its bloodiest examples of the Counter-Reformation . . . The air itself, suffused with the ponderous rain, reflected a light that could not be completely of the here and now because while its sheen lay on everything, the source of the light was impossible to detect under the heavy blanket of cloud.

On the upper, broader end of the square, across from the plague column, a fountain threw thin, elegant streams, about 3 metres into the air that formed spuming arcs before falling back to earth. This was no powerful jet of water but, rather, a genteel spray that could barely hold its own against the rain's sluggish patter. The fountain was newly installed at the centre of a circle, with verses from a poem by Jan Skácel written in its concentric rings on the ground, from the centre outward.

It was admirable that of all verses the Brno city council had chosen Skácel's, since he had declared in an article that not one of the many fountains in Brno served the purpose fountains are intended to, filled as they were with all sorts of things, like 'paint and cooking oil cans, wilted flowers', instead of what they're actually supposed to be filled with: water. The new fountain, therefore, was going to be different—free from trash and filled with clean, flowing water—and was dedicated to the poet who died in Brno in 1989.

We sat in a cafe, watching what the Brno rain was up to, and I pestered my travelling companion with a story that had been on my mind for a long time: the story of the poet, whom many of the poets of Brno esteem as the greatest among them and who died twice. Ivan Blatný was born here in 1919 and worked at in an optician's shop on Česká, Czech Street, which runs almost up to Freedom Square. In opposition to the Nazi occupying forces, he wrote a spray of fine poems in which it is almost always raining and almost always November.

Adieu, in the streets of my love
the rain does not let up
the metal of the signs rattles on
it washes the wrinkles from the old neighbourhood
without end.

Blatný considered himself a supporter of the 'ordinary and unremarkable man' and an unremarkable man with his ordinary happiness is what he himself wanted to be. Four of his books were published when he was only twenty-five; he was not even thirty when he died the first time.

Writing poetry, he said, is nothing other than 'noticing how one's steps on the sand-covered paths in the park sound different after the rain'. In 1948, this highly praised *wunderkind* with an alarmingly fine-tuned sensory perception arrived in England in a delegation of Czech writers. There the group received the news that the Stalinists had crushed the anti-fascist popular front and had assumed total power. Blatný did not want to obey the command to return immediately, presumably in order to receive instructions in conformity with the new political situation. When his friends and colleagues were ready to leave from Ipswich, one member of their delegation was missing. They searched for him for a few hours, then wrote him off. Ivan Blatný did not resurface. He made no anti-Communist statements, he did not appear in émigré circles, he had disappeared without a trace. After two years, he was declared officially deceased in Czechoslovakia.

Twenty years later, he was found. Blatný had spent the years after his defection from the group and disappearance in an English mental asylum and when a relative came to visit him, he found an old man with wild hair and a flickering look in his eyes. It's thanks to a nurse that this man who had been dead for twenty years began to write again. She collected and saved what he scribbled on slips of paper that she would set out for him, and one day she sent them off to the legendary publishing house, Sixty-Eight Publishers, run in Toronto by the writer Josef Škvorecký who had fled in 1968 after the next *putsch* led by outside forces in Czechoslovakia. Blatný had twenty more years left to him and he would spend them in St Clement's Hospital in Ipswich composing strangely lucid poems. He wrote that fear was constantly perched inside him, the 'fear of fists and kicks', and offered a summary of himself that is steeped in Brno sadness but devoid of self-pity: 'What a shame that I had to live in fear.'

In his late poetry, he steps out of the desolate, ruined landscape of his life and returns to the streets of Brno glistening with rain in eternal November: 'And now I will fall silent, Adieu, November came.' In August 1990, he died a second time.

In homage to Blatný, a different Czech poet changed his name to Listopad, which means November in Czech. I first learnt of this other poet when I stopped in Ottensheim on the Danube on my way to Moravia in order to get advice for my trip from the wood engraver, Christian Thanhäuser, who had long been exploring Bohemia and Moravia. One day, when Jiří Synek's friend Blatný, whose literary forte was November, did not return and Synek himself was living in another country fenced in by a foreign language, he decided to change his name to František Listopad. He is Blatný's brother in spirit, his happier, more boisterous sibling, protected by an indestructibly cheerful rebelliousness. Listopad followed the same literary and political paths as Blatný, but when he arrived at the crossroads, he had the freedom to choose another direction.

Two years younger than Blatný, Listopad published six volumes of poetry in breathtakingly rapid succession in early 1945 under his birth name. His writing combined radical social criticism with delight in aesthetic experimentation, a test of the alliance of socialism and surrealism, an alliance which would later take on the different form of a grim fatality. The young author was one of the founders of the journal *Mladá Fronta* (Young Front) and when he, at twenty-six, was offered the position of Paris correspondent in 1947, he departed immediately. He did not see his homeland again until he was an old man because the news reached him in Paris a few months after his arrival, as it had his friend Ivan in Ipswich, that the brief period of openness was over and that of enforced Socialist development had begun. Listopad, who did not yet go by the name, had made his entrance as a poet of 'the little people' who know that they are 'always threatened by the deluge from above' and therefore try to behave as rebellious insurgents in everyday life and not as obedient Party soldiers. They not only fight for social justice but also for beauty and elegance, like the 'coalman' who never leaves the dismal cellar hole without a 'carnation on his lapel'.

Listopad stayed in Paris for four years, then went to Portugal where for four decades he taught various subjects in many universities until he was named head of that country's only film school. No one in Portugal knew that this respected man was a Czech poet and no one in Czechoslovakia knew that the unruly genius of a long-forgotten era was still alive. But like Blatný, who had taken refuge in an English mental asylum, Synek was alive, though now as Listopad, a figure in Portuguese intellectual life who blessed his homeland with six Czech-Portuguese children. When he thought of home, the man who called himself November always thought of the rain that connected the essential sadness of Portugal, freed from all personal embellishment, with Bohemia:

Portuguese rain
sounds pink
a Bohemian sound
in each drop

In 1990, the year Blatný died in England, Listopad returned to Bohemia and Moravia. As an emeritus Portuguese academic, he immediately took up his work as a Czech poet again and published twelve books in the breathtakingly rapid succession of his youth. He completed his literary homecoming by visiting landscapes and cities he had not seen since he was young in methodical reminiscence of his former companions. Sitting in a cafe this long-lost man learnt of the death of his long-lost friend from whose poems he had taken his name. What is the first thing he thinks of?

Ivan is dead, I read in the paper
sitting next to Madame Eliška's pillar.
What if it rained? And drops immediately began to fall . . .

Lost Souls, Saved Bodies:
Brno, Špilberk, the Capuchin Crypt

The woefully thin tinkling of the Hare Krishnas' bells accompanies them as they make their way through Catholic Brno, rapt in the singsong that consists, for the duration of their spiritual life, of the same two words in exactly the same sequence of notes. Anyone who does nothing but repeat them over and over again while dancing and tapping a tambourine will lose his mind after one morning or two weeks, if he hasn't already. But it seems to me that someone must already have lost his mind before making his way with chanting and pealing bells through cities that are nothing more to him than a collection of paths he must follow, singing, to attain utmost bliss. In any case we could not escape them, the two men, four women and three children who, through some mysterious providence, kept appearing before us when we hoped we'd left them behind.

In the large and lively Zelný trh, the vegetable market square, in the centre of which preens the Parnassus Fountain—Fischer von Erlach's most hideous construction; the unparalleled master of the Baroque must have been in a dark mood when he designed it and wanting to cock a snook at the ornate style—the Hare Krishnas came towards us hopping and whirling. An hour earlier, at the other end of the historic city centre, we had fled from them into the Red Church in the well-founded hope that they, in their orange robes, wouldn't want to follow us inside. But in front of the hulking, downright fleshy limestone fountain with its supposed natural grotto beside which are perched three stout allegorical figures from the ancient empires of Babylon, Persia and Greece, they found us again. The few hundred locals buying vegetables at the market were apparently used to them because they scarcely looked up at the Hare Krishnas dancing, dead-eyed and absent in their bliss, along the rows of stands, as if they had no idea whether they were in Brno, Ouagadougou or Madison.

Later in the day, when we heard their tinkling bells in another part of town, we slipped into a narrow, shady street that ran along the left side of the Capuchin monastery and opened onto a quiet square. There you find the entrance to Brno's Capuchin Crypt, which offers a more memorable experience than the sealed, plague-infected coffins of the Habsburgs in Vienna. I had not planned on visiting the Brno crypt since I believe it sacrilege to display the dead to the eyes of the living. However, in order to rescue myself from the living who drone on soullessly, I sought out the dead who had not managed to disappear from the earth after their souls and spirits had fled.

Ever since I survived Sélestat, I'd been on guard not to end up unintentionally in circumstances that some people enjoy, namely, of looking at the dead whom museums find all kinds of excuses to display for gaping visitors. Once a human being has been dead long enough, does he or she count as one of the things or objects anyone can dig up, clean, drape and put in a display case for the sake of necrophiliac delight or some scientific whim? And yet, there I was in a famous crypt, a spiritual gallery of the departed whose corpses were not allowed to decay in the ground but were kept on hand for pious contemplation.

The Capuchin Monastery was founded just after 1600 and the church was built around it fifty years later. The Capuchins were the Counter-Reformation's friendly tool. They did not come with swords to persuade the godforsaken Protestants with striking arguments to convert to the true faith. Instead, they arrived barefoot and clad in the brown hairshirt robes of beggars and founded hospitals, almshouses and orphanages. They visited the unfortunate whom the Catholic state had thrown in prison and, carrying a cross, accompanied those condemned of patricide, highway robbery or unrepentant heresy to their executions. Beneath the altar in their beautiful church only modestly adorned with works of art, they excavated a vault that served them as crypt in which the monks and several citizens of Brno who had assisted the order in their mission of recatholicization or in the construction of the church and monastery. Due to the special geological composition of the stone and the sophisticated system of ventilation, the bodies buried in the crypt did not decay but instead were mummified. More than 200 bodies were deposited within cool, dark masonry and 41 of their mummified bodies were preserved. In them and their gaping mouths, open for a silent, final scream echoing through eternity, visitors can recognize themselves and a future that will come soon enough.

The most famous of these figures who were once men of flesh and blood but are now withered into a kind of brown straw has his own room—the very first room in the crypt. In a metal coffin with a glass lid lies a soldier who turned pious at the end of his life and paid for burial with the mendicant friars of the Capuchin order with the wealth he had amassed in the service of her majesty, the Empress Maria Theresia. Baron Franz von der Trenck, presented in a movie based on his life as a daring, gallant adventurer, was the commander of a corps of irregulars who rampaged on the orders of the Habsburgs wherever a rebellious population needed to be brought to reason or a stalled military advance needed to be prompted back into motion through ambush and massacre. The frightful reputation of the Pandurs, as this unit was called, ran ahead of them and in their wake, they left a trail of smoking debris, maimed bodies and violated women. They were convicts and violent criminals freed expressly for this destruction; they were given free rein over the conquered and their possessions.

For years, the baron, who had murdered the sons of countless mothers and handed over the daughters to his Pandurs, knew he enjoyed the motherly empress's special favour. But somehow or other—some claim a joke at her expense, others brazen embezzlement—he squandered the empress's good graces. He was thrown into the monarchy's most notorious prison in the Špilberk fortress in

Brno. During the three years he spent there, chained to a wall, death penetrated his bones and he, the powerful fellow, melted into one single desire: to leave this world as quickly as possible for a better one. He bequeathed the wealth he still possessed to the Capuchins, who collected his body from Špilberk when he died at thirty-seven and buried him in the crypt under their altar.

His body is slender and the struts of his clavicle are visible through the shroud. Trenck must have been a large man. The head, however, is too small for this body and, in fact, it is not his. His head had been severed after he died and probably sent to his relatives as evidence or a family relic. So that his body wouldn't lie there without a head, the monks cut off the head of one of their deceased brothers and laid it in the coffin of this merciless war hero, mercilessly punished prisoner, and sinner who found mercy in death. There the head lies, teeth exposed under the lips worn away over the centuries in a terrible grin.

I had visited Špilberk fortress the day before. I'd wanted to see with my own eyes the place I'd heard a story about many years before, a story that is equally horrifying and pathetic and, however much the sources maintain it is true, completely unbelievable: the story of Alexandre Andryane, a wealthy young man from Lyon inspired by the ideal of European revolution who was sent to Špilberk where he began writing a study of the 'nature of humanity'. When his ink was confiscated, he drew some of his own blood and, undaunted, continued to write in praise of free humanity.

Špilberk mountain is a relatively steep but not very high elevation that rises in the centre of Brno. On top is a structure that was first built in the thirteenth century and altered many times to serve various purposes: initially as a medieval residence, later an almost impenetrable fortified castle, always as a jail for political prisoners reinforced with military barracks and a tremendous armoury. The name of the mountain soon stood for the barracks and finally for the prison itself, from which the Habsburg Monarchy in turn was given the nickname 'Völkerkerker' or 'Prison of Nations' by its enemies. This nickname certainly suited the Špilberk prison as well because the most dangerous rebels from every country in the monarchy were incarcerated there, such that around c.1800 it held Hungarian Jacobins who dreamt of civilian revolution, Polish patriots who wanted to restore their fatherland which had been crushed with Austria's assistance and Italian Carbonari who were fighting for the unification of Italy. They rotted alive in the casemates or the vast vaults dug underground as a military shelter that were subsequently used to punish prisoners in eternal darkness. The inmates stood in ankle-deep water, bound in chains or even clamped directly to the walls—most only survived a few months in Špilberk. Legend has it that Emperor Joseph II, the most enlightened of the Habsburg monarchs, visited the prison and found all the prisoners at death's door or driven insane. Appalled, he ordered the prison be shut down as he left. After his death, however, it was expanded and continued to swallow prisoners until 1846 when the Krakow insurgents were sent there.

In the end, progress turns prisons into museums. The museum on the hill of Brno doesn't address the horror these barracks, this place of torture, represent. On the plateau, the visitor passes through the exceptionally well restored fortifications which offer a magnificent view of the city. Even in the casements, the visitor is spared any sense of horror, since they are so carefully maintained and swept clean of dirt. When the guide rattled off the history of the site, as if he had found his own professional 'Hare Krishna' for a few dozen tourists from different countries, his topic seemed very far removed from him and from the visitors he briskly led through the site to the museum restaurant.

For decades, Jan Vilhem von Zinzendorf was commander of Špilberk, lord of the barracks and the prison, commanding officer of the soldiers who practised their drills in the ramparts and the unfettered tormenter of the prisoners languishing in the fortress' vaults. In 1685, this God-fearing man died, loyal to his emperor, graced with worldly honours and comforted with spiritual consolation. According to his humble desire, he was welcomed into the Capuchins' realm of the dead. With six others, he lies in the fourth room of the crypt, his head bent slightly back and to the side, his mouth wide open as if he were screaming out one of the agonies he so abundantly inflicted on others but didn't know how to cope with himself. Next to him his daughter-in-law Isabella lies contorted on her daybed, her delicate body twisted in terrible death throes, her head pressed onto her left shoulder, her hands clenched; it is assumed that she suffered from a contagious disease, was considered dead and immediately buried— alive—just as the prisoners who rotted in her father-in-law's deadly realm.

In the sixth and last room of the crypt, the Capuchins themselves are buried. One hundred and fifty monks were carried down from the church to the crypts by candlelight by their fellow monks. They always used the same coffin with a wooden bottom that could be pulled back for the corpse to slip out of the coffin and onto the vault's stone floor. Capuchin equality reigned in the crypt: the abbot lies next to the gardener; all the monks have their arms crossed over their collapsed chests in the same way; one has lost his teeth; another has lost his nasal bones; the arc and ridge of a third's eyebrows are still unsettlingly clear. They lie in the dust, skulls resting on bricks for eternity. On the back wall of the room hang a cross and two plaques on which is carved what the mummified Capuchins have to teach those who have come to see them: *Co js.'e vy—byli jsme my, co jsme my—budete i vy.* They teach that their bones, which time has not completely divested of flesh, are our future: 'As you are now—we once were; as we are now—you shall be.'

Svoboda, the Humanist (The Neo-Latinists IV)

In the first half of the eighteenth century in Prague, there lived a man who dreamt of morally improving mankind and of establishing peace between the Germans and the Czechs, a man who, driven by the mildest of intentions, lost his mind. He tirelessly corresponded with scholars around the world, researched in archives, wrote studies, published documents from the early history of the German and Czech nations, which affected his health almost without his noticing. He died of overwork at the age of forty-nine, which ultimately exempted him from attending the meetings of the numerous educational associations and committees he had either founded or revitalized. His fiftieth birthday was commemorated in Prague with dignity and he, who had once dreamt of uniting many countries in peace under one language, was once again spoken of in many languages in the press throughout the entire Danube monarchy.

Václav Alois Svoboda was considered a linguistic genius and the old books that reference him here and there rarely fail to mention that he was able to speak and write at least twelve languages. At the same time, this man wanted to impart knowledge of world poetry to those who lacked any gift for languages. As a translator, Svoboda left behind a vast body of work evidencing an impressive feeling for language that, admittedly, hardly anyone is in a position to read. For Svoboda did not seek to translate poetry into the language of living people but into the eternity of Latin. He therefore studied Czech, Romanian and Ruthenian folk poetry to present them to Europeans in Latin anthologies. His linguistic masterwork was the *Selecta Frederici Schiller Carmina Rhythmis Latinis*, a collection of ballads, hymns and poems by the classic German author. The few who were in a position to judge it agreed that in the entire nineteenth century no one wrote such vibrant Latin as Svoboda, the Bohemian humanist.

CHAPTER SEVEN

Lost in Bucureşti: Bulevardul Mihail Kogălniceanu

The first thing I heard in the morning, just before seven, was the laughter of a few women approaching, accompanied by a peculiar swishing sound, soon the swishing and the laughter moved off again. I got up and looked out of the greasy-yellow net curtains on the second floor of the Hotel Academica and saw a cleaning brigade of six Roma women in greenish-yellow uniforms using gnarled brooms with thick bunches of dried twigs for bristles to sweep the pavement. Over the next days, I would see them everywhere in the city, these crews of Romani, incessantly cleaning the streets of Bucharest so that even at night you could walk home on clean-swept pavements and need only take care not to step into an open manhole.

Hotel Academica was located on the vast grounds of the law school—it was not exactly a park, but neither was it an expanse sprinkled with piles of prefabricated buildings. Instead, the grounds were a mixture of both with a particular shabby charm. Here the institute's professors, students and guests lived separated but still as neighbours and the patches of grass between their blocks of flats were sparsely furnished with tables and benches. The student residences, the dining hall, the university buildings with lecture halls and the faculty apartments were connected by pavements and narrow streets that were cleaned each morning with brooms and peals of laughter.

The Universitatea de Drept was on the Bulevardul Mihail Kogălniceanu which led from the city centre past the Cişmigiu Park, generously adorned with ponds and beds of native and exotic flowers, to the new opera. Cars roared along this road at excessive speeds every hour of the day or night and even the stray dogs—about whom I'd been warned because so many are rabid and sometimes rise woozily from the dirt only to bite the leg of a passer-by quick as a flash—even the dogs had learnt from the fate of their fellows run over in traffic that crossing the boulevard was a mortal danger. The first time I took up position on the kerb to wait for one of the gaps in the traffic that appear every few minutes through which I could scurry to the other side, suddenly two mangy, limping, timorous beasts appeared next to me. They had slunk up as if they knew how bad their reputation was. One was spotted greyish-white and the fur on its back was abraded down to the skin; the other was a curious-looking, elongated, dejected black animal whose stomach scraped the ground when it walked. They waited until I set off at a run and stayed close to my side until we reached the other side. Then one of the two disappeared with spry leaps into a side street and the other trotted unhurriedly up the Bulevardul as if he wanted to check on the state of affairs on this side.

I had flown in from Timişoara the day before. At the airport, a burly taxi driver approached with a friendly air, snatched up my bag and, in this manner, invited me without ado to follow him to his car. He was a stocky, bald man in his fifties whose neck bulged in three red, inflamed folds. When we were stopped in traffic on the multi-laned Calea Bucurestilor, I asked him if he could close the window because the rain had become so heavy that we were both getting drenched inside the car. No, he said with regret, it isn't possible because the air would be too bad if he had to smoke with the windows closed. It had been sunny in Timişoara that morning, but the plane soon entered a white, grey and nearly black bank of clouds. It shook and rattled non-stop and when I caught the stewardess' eye, she gave me an automatic smile although her eyes were wide with horror. I asked myself what on earth I was doing in this plane and if, perhaps, what I was seeking in Romania was death.

After we advanced yet again a few hundred metres before coming to a standstill, the driver, Horia, offered me a cigarette and asked where I came from. When I told him, we had a topic of conversation. Two days earlier, the Austrian national football team had surprisingly beat the Romanians, a fact that confirmed how rotten the world was because the Romanian footballers were paid too much—the same claim was made about the Austrians—and it ruined their character. Horia could judge; he and his wife got around. They'd always preferred Italy. There they understood the language, as if they were visiting relatives, and watching the matches in the elegant stadiums of Milan, Florence and Turin was pure pleasure.

But for some time, Horia had stopped travelling to his favourite country. The Italians had become racist, he explained, and the way they treated his countrymen, the Romani from Romania was a disgrace for Europe. It was also a disgrace that Europe didn't even consider calling Italy to account. Such a beautiful country, such beautiful football stadiums and such an idiot as a leader! The muscles of his swollen face twitched involuntarily with waves of indignation which agitated his body as well as his sensitive soul. I eagerly assured him that I found Berlusconi every bit the European disgrace that he did. But that stumped Horia. He thought hard then shook his head: No, not Berlusconi, he's the one with the sports channel, but the other.

He couldn't remember who the other one was who embodied all the ill of the formerly good Italy and instead entertained me the entire long trip into the city by describing all the famous football players he'd seen and memorable events he'd witnessed on the fields: toppled goal posts, rain-soaked battles, unjustified or all too justified ejections, cunning free kicks, a referee who suffered a heart attack during a game, and two teams in the second division who didn't resume play after half-time but quit because they weren't enjoying the game. Mussolini, he shouted suddenly, Mussolini is the dog who's the reason why decent lovers of football can't travel to Italy any more. When we arrived at the law school, he took my suitcase from the boot of the car and carried it 100 metres from the street to the hotel with great solicitude as if to justify his audacious advance at the airport. In the following days I often regretted not having asked him for his telephone number because that first taxi driver was the only one who showed any concern for me.

The stretch from the hotel to the old city (and later back again) was too long to be a pleasure to cover two, four or six times a day on foot but it was too short a distance to have a taxi standing by to drive me the kilometre and a half. For the entire week I didn't find a single taxi willing to drive me from the city along the Bulevardul Kogăl-niceanu to my lodgings. For the four lei the distance would have cost to cover, the drivers didn't even want to turn on the motor and they refused the ten lei I offered them instead, for which they'd have had to drive around the neighbourhood for at least a quarter of an hour because asking for a higher fare than was justified offended their sense of honour. And so, they left me on my own at all hours of the day and night, in the rain and in the heatwave that suddenly washed over the city on the fourth day while they sat in their cars smoking out the open window, idle and unpaid.

One afternoon, as I was heading back to my hotel on Bulevardul Kogălniceanu—plodding along absent-mindedly in my exhaustion—I crossed a chubby young woman carrying a student satchel who was waddling from the law school towards the city centre. As she came closer, I saw that tears were flowing down her reddened cheeks, deeply scarred by years of severe acne; her attention turned inward, she strode through the city as through her grief: immersed in her own thoughts and closed off to her surroundings. She wept continuously without sobbing; she wept her way home and would only burst out into loud sobs when she had closed the door behind her. I stepped aside and turned back after she had passed me, and I noticed a plaque I had overlooked before. It was mounted 3 metres above the ground on a handsome neoclassical townhouse with a yellow-orange facade and many oriel windows that would have fit right in on a Parisian street lined with trees. This is where the writer Tudor Arghezi lived from 1912 to 1930, that is until his thirty-second year. Here he wrote *The Wooden Icons*, pensive and heretical sketches in which he depicted, with religious fervour and despair, life in the orthodox monastery to which he had fled in his youth and from which he escaped a few years later.

I didn't know which affected me more deeply, the weeping of the young woman who was leaving the unhappiness of the university for the unhappiness of home or the plaque honouring the dead poet whom I hadn't been looking for but who had long been part of my personal, imaginary Europe. To spare myself the misplaced choice between the sorrowful life and literature that is able to preserve sorrow for all eternity while at the same time transcending it through language, I decided it was the coincidence of the two: I would never have discovered the poet's house if not for the sad young woman who had perhaps just failed an exam at the university that Arghezi had portrayed in a bitter, caustic novel as an academic realm of the dead, a domain of ghosts and revenants.

After a few days in Bucharest, I took provisional stock of my adventure in this city: taxi drivers refused to drive me, even when I wanted to bribe them and make it worth their while; the only one who took me under his wing with ruthless friendliness looked like a bouncer and his gentle disposition gave way to rage only when he thought of the reprehensible racism and greed that held sway throughout the world. The constantly sweeping Romani, who, according to propaganda spread across the country, were taking advantage of social welfare to support their parasitical existence, seemed to be the only ones actually working in the capital and as if in mockery, they did their work as if it were the most fun they could possibly have. Trembling, the rabid dogs cowered in the dirt. They were docile and, of all people, they chose me, afraid of dogs all my life, as a protector. I could not find the book of mine that Humanitas Press had published in any of the numerous branches of the publisher's own bookshop chain. When I asked a sales assistant in the main store next to Kretzulescu Church on Revolution Square, she searched in the computer for a long time, picked up the telephone receiver to enquire with the publisher and was forwarded to one person after another in an apparently enormous company before finally informing me consolingly that the book wouldn't appear for another three months. That same day, however, in a different bookshop in the city, one that was not owned by the publisher, I did find a copy in the bargain bin with the rest of the unsellable stock.

On the way back to my hotel from the city, where such was my reality, I would often take a rest in Cișmigiu Park, not far from Hotel Academica and read the Mihail Kogălniceanu biography I had bought. He was an immensely erudite, bold, big-hearted man who prepared the liberal politicians for the glorious yet failed 1848 Revolution, in which civil liberty and the union of the Romanian principalities were at stake. In his memoirs he wrote that his sheltered childhood and adolescence were darkened by the suffering he observed but could not do anything about. People 'with chains on their arms and legs' and others with 'metal collars around their necks' were herded through the streets and, if they resisted, were flogged, left lying bloodied in roadside ditches or in winter even thrown in icy rivers. From his youth, Kogălniceanu studied the language and customs of these chained people who did not lose their insolent laughter or defiant looks and in the provocative pamphlet 'Emancipation of the Gypsies', written when he was twenty-seven; he demanded the abolition of the enforced system of Romani bondage in Bessarabia, Walachia and Moldavia in which they were categorized as *Robi domnești, Robi boierești* and *Robi manaștiresti*, unfree people of the crown, unfree people of the bojars or landowners and unfree people of the monasteries. In Tudor Arghezi's novel *The Buna Vestire Cemetery*, published in 1933, three years after he had moved from Bulevardul Kogălniceanu to the suburbs, Mihail Kogălniceanu, who had died in 1891, can no longer bear being confined in his grave and so he rises from the dead to make sure that everything in Romania is in order. But before he can revive the passive revolution, he is immediately arrested and sent to prison in Văcărești.

To Văcăreşti: A Visit to Tudor Arghezi

In his Swiftian *Tablets from the Land of Kuty*, a dystopian satire, Tudor Arghezi sends his protagonist on a fanciful expedition through a country that is a model of true democracy. This futuristic kingdom is built on three pillars: the phenomenal stupidity of its statesmen, the indestructible opportunism of its state artists and the narrow-mindedness of its government officials who exist in a kind of bureaucratic delirium, dreaming of regulations, decrees and edicts.

Then one of the politicians who tirelessly strives to improve the state of affairs and organize the body politic more intelligently has an idea that is unusually ingenious and bold even for Kuty, itself an empire of ingenious plans and bold visions. Cities, expressions in stone of the human propensity for anarchy and chaos, could surely be better arranged, more logically designed if reason were the primary organizing principle of urban development. And so a plan is made to dismantle the cities and rebuild them, grouping similar parts together, resulting in the ultimate, beneficial urban system: a district only for churches, an area with nothing but water pipes, a large section of the city where all the roads had senselessly led hither and tither would be systematically planned, a district with monuments—whether riders on horseback or uniformed men on two feet—neatly lined up next to each other ...

In 1933, Tudor Arghezi published *Tablets from the Land of Kuty*, the parody of a state in which the common good is invoked all the more emphatically, the more meaningless it is. His criticism was aimed at the notorious 'conditions in Romania' between the wars with the nation-wide corruption, the small-minded provincials' delusions of grandeur and the methodical fogging of the subjects' minds with nationalist incense. His contempt for those who craved status could not have been more ferocious. Half a century later, the satire could have as easily been sparked by Ceaușescu's enlightened plans for 'agro-industrial concentration' and the 'village systematization'. Yet when the Conducător set about reducing his country precisely to modern Dacian ruins, this text was buried in the author's voluminous collected works.

Arghezi died in 1967 at a very advanced age and celebrated as a national poet, an honour he earned late in life and with more than one compromise. Until the last decade of his life, he had always despised the state and its changing authorities and offices. During the First World War, in which Romanians fought the united monarchies of the Hohenzollern and the Habsburgs, he was branded 'pro-German' because of his pacifist writings and thrown in the Văcărești prison in south-eastern Bucharest. During the Second World War, however, when Romania was on the side of the Third Reich, his 'anti-German' pamphlets were grounds for deporting him to the Târgu Jiu internment camp. There is no doubt—Arghezi had a talent for doing the right thing at the wrong time. Arghezi was ostracized after the war as well, when Romanian society was being suppressed and the state was being Stalinized. In his ninth decade, however, he was discovered by the state authorities and proclaimed a national poet, and the elderly Arghezi acquiesced to this extorted reconciliation. Many in future generations resented him for this and would have found it more elegant if, instead of being admitted to the pantheon, the eighty-year-old had been sent to prison one last time. Nevertheless, his work is also a reservoir of revolt that is still far from depleted.

Arghezi's *oeuvre* comprises all genres and forms. In his militant journalism, Arghezi did not limit himself to denouncing abuses in general but, rather, he gave the names and titles of those for whom corruption was a profitable business and mendacity their official language. His short prose is absurdly witty, full of linguistic capers and a frantic play of associations that borders on the Surrealistic, a specifically Romanian characteristic to which many writers, important in that country but hardly known in the West—from Urmuz to Gellu Naum—paid poetic tribute. Arghezi's dark and yet laugh-out-loud comical novels, of which *The Buna Vestire Cemetery* is the darkest and funniest, are an academic danse macabre in which the living are deader than dead and so enshrined in convention and stupidity that the dead have no choice but to come back to life. Arghezi emphatically wanted these sarcastic works to be considered poems. His literary works span the range from rhythmic folk songs to reflective poetry, from evocations of the lost world of childhood rich with imagery and intense colours to laconic notes on many sounds written in his prison cell. As a poet, Arghezi took up almost every possible theme at some point or other—death, love, religion, the cycle of nature, the rhythm of the metropolis. There's only one theme you will search for in vain in his work: the kind of poem included in enormous anthologies of patriotic verse from all people and eras to the astonishment and dismay of later generations.

He published his first poems at the age of sixteen, and at nineteen, he sought refuge from difficult living circumstances and inner torment in the Cernica Monastery not far from Bucharest. He remained a mystic his entire life, even after he had renounced a future as an Orthodox monk and thrown himself furiously into the political conflicts of his time. Like many poets of small nations with few democratic traditions to build on, Arghezi was tempted, time and again, to set his writing table up defiantly on the street. The local heavies were too numerous and seemed too ludicrous in their grandiosity for him to resist attempting to undermine their power with his words. All his life he longed to withdraw and live compassionately on the margins. Yet, he wrote thousands of newspaper opinion pieces—some fiercely indignant and others filled with an icy contempt that still gives readers shivers—and was constantly engaged with various journal projects. One of these, called *Facla*, was a blazing reflection of Karl Kraus' magazine *Die Fackel*, a torch kept lit in Vienna. Later, with *Bilete de papagal* (Parrot Tickets), Arghezi produced a satirical newspaper almost single-handedly. The title referred to a fortune-telling tradition at Romanian fairs, where for a few lei a parrot pulls scraps of paper with prophecies out of a box.

The district of Văcărești, in the southern part of Bucharest, can be reached from the centre via the long Șoseaua Olteniței road. This avenue initially leads past shopping centres and small businesses, then past several cemeteries, before the Strada Mărțișor forks off to the right. This street's name comes from the 'little March' that many Romanians offer each other as a gift on the first of March: a white-and-red string on which hangs a luck charm, a golden heart, a small token of love. Tall apartment buildings loom on one side of Strada Mărțișor, the other is lined with modest single-family homes of elderly citizens who managed to hold on to their property through the communist decades and recently constructed ostentatious villas in every possible architectural style. Seventy years ago, fields and pastures covered the area with only two buildings in the vicinity: the Văcărești Monastery, which had been transformed into the notorious prison, and the community abattoir. Tudor Arghezi bought himself a plot here and in 1930 began building a house with the assistance of architect friend, G. M. Cantacuzino. He called the house Mărțișor, or little March, and built an annexe for a small printing press to publish *Parrot Tickets* with their predictions.

An old woman wearing a uniform-like skirt and jacket is waiting in the garden. She sizes me up with mild severity as if she would admit me regardless but would rather discover something about me first that proved me worthy of admittance to her childhood home. Mițura's look cleared when I introduced myself because, as she explained with growing friendliness, I was the first Austrian visitor to the Tudor Arghezi Museum in Mărțișor. There was an air of rebuke in her reply that didn't apply to me but to the nation that I suddenly represented, a nation that rightly should have sent an emissary long ago. But still, each year the house had 6,000 visitors, even if most were students brought on school trips from all over the country to see the house of the man after whom countless Romanian schools are named.

This house had a white facade and red doors and shutters—a 'little March' indeed—and a peculiar design with wood verandas and two small towers that made it look like a small mansion with a half-folkloric, half-modernist air. The story goes that Arghezi had chosen this spot so his wife Paraschiva would not have far to go should she again need to visit him in the Văcărești prison, where his lack of literary patriotism had already landed him once. Most of the photographs of him on display in the museum showed the delinquent as a distinguished elderly gentleman with white hair and a meticulously groomed moustache, whose determined chin and gaze were nonetheless blurred and turned inwards. He wore a dark suit and bowtie and held a walking stick that was less a support than the indispensable accessory of a dandy to whom it would never have occurred to leave the house without one. In almost every photograph, a stocky, black-haired woman stands at the elegant gentleman's side. She was more grounded than he and less dreamy, as if it were incumbent on her to spy out the dangers that lurked on every side, and to move them out of his way.

In every room, the museum tried to give the impression that Arghezi had only just left and was expected back any minute. Every object seemed to be waiting for him, his spectacles and the fountain pen on his desk, the beautifully worn leather satchel leaning on the armchair next to the walking stick with a black winter cap hanging on the handle. Everything was set up and spread out to create a specific illusion that time had stopped and, were it suddenly to start again, it would resume its ephemeral work in 1967—the year in which the owner died and left all these possessions behind. Even his slippers were set out side by side before the sofa in such a way that the imaginary inhabitant of this moribund house could slip his feet into them at any time—if he would but return from the dead, like the protagonist of his novel *The Buna Vestire Cemetery*. The dining-room table was set as if dinner would be served in ten minutes of eternity and the old gramophone in the parlour was loaded with a record—Wagner's *Tannhäuser*—waiting only for someone to turn the handle so it could begin to play.

In the attic nursery, time seemed to be waiting even more expectantly than in the other rooms. A resolute elderly woman led me into the room where she had lined up her childhood dolls and when she glanced at me from the corner of her eye, curious to hear my reaction to the room, the dolls and the neatly arranged toys, I was struck by the uncertainty in her gaze, the hunger for praise and approval; hers was the look of a child who is proud of her possessions and eager to hear that she has reason to be proud. Then I realized that Miţura was an eighty-year-old child, the eternal, favourite daughter of the greatest Romanian poet of the Modern age.

If you wanted a comparison for Arghezi's poetry, that of the Austrian Theodor Kramer might serve. He and Arghezi share a sympathy for the marginalized, for the inferior things of daily life, and both felt that their fame and laurels belonged to the shabby, less noteworthy side of life. And Arghezi, like Kramer, found dignity and beauty not in the world of the comfortable and the complacent but in the arduous daily grind of the poor, in creaturely misery, and in barren landscapes rather than in pleasant ones:

My heart's a rain-swept road,
A road with dust and sheep,
Barren road between trees,
Vineyard skew-whiff on poles,
Village with dogs, yards,
Ash from furrows and ploughs.
Herd grazing the land,
Scurry of crows in the wind,
Buffalo half out of mud,
Heavy head
Gazing at great emptiness.

—'Song on a Flute'

'Of Whom Europe Knows Nothing...':
Rosetti, Rosenthal, Margul-Sperber

The greatest Romanian patriot was a Hungarian Jew who was tortured to death in a Habsburg prison. Constantin Daniel Rosenthal was twenty-two the first time he went to Romania—though it didn't

IN THE FOREST OF METROPOLES

yet exist in 1842 and was only created twenty years later with the union of the two principalities of Wallachia and Moldavia—which had initially been under Ottoman rule, then under Russian influence. Rosenthal was immediately smitten with the country, considered one of the most backwards in Europe at the time, and with the capital city, which had to be periodically rebuilt because of earthquakes and fires and then, following a series of catastrophes, became the Balkan metropolis of modern architecture. But that was later, for the Budapest-born Rosenthal arrived in Bucharest in 1842 after studying at the Academy of Fine Arts in Vienna. He soon became passionate about the concerns of the Wallachian revolutionaries and as a result always returned from his study trips in France and England to the land that had the historical misfortune of being located where three great powers collided: the Ottoman Empire, Tsarist Russia and the Habsburg Empire.

These powers' hostility towards each other did not prevent them from working together to prevent the disputed principalities from gaining independence. They joined forces to crush the Wallachian Revolution of 1848. Anyone wanting to keep his liberal head on his own shoulders had to flee. One of these was Constantin Rosenthal who landed in Paris where he dreamt of a Wallachian national uprising.

In 1850 in Paris, he painted his best-known work, 'Revolutionary Romania', which is depicted as a young woman with long, dark hair falling over both shoulders, clothed in a colourful Wallachian folk costume that owes more to his imagination than tradition. She has a long, straight, narrow nose, under which her mouth is defiantly shut. She gazes resolutely into a future that will bring equal rights, gender equality and the abolition of bondage. Maria Rosetti personified all of this. For Rosenthal, her face represented the Romanian revolution.

This icon of the revolution, painted by a Hungarian Jew, depicts an Englishwoman who dreamt of the unity of the Romanian fatherland as ardently as the painter. The movement for the unification of all Romanian-inhabited lands was the work of cosmopolitans—very few of them from that region—who proclaimed the idea of national unity with a thoroughly worldly pathos and who believed the uprisings across the continent to be a European issue that concerned everyone. Indeed, they saw the revolutions that were intended to sweep away rotting feudal despotism from even the most remote provinces as laying the foundation of a new Europe in which nation states were not an end but a path towards freedom. Mary Grant was the daughter of an English shipowner and a French woman. Her husband, the liberal writer and politician Constantin Alexandru Rosetti, was a descendant of the despised Phanariots, the prominent Greek families in Constantinople from whose ranks the Ottomans recruited their most important officials, officers and administrators. Their renown as nearly mythological figures of Romanian unity can be attributed to the French historian Jules Michelet, who devoted a book to them, and to the brilliant young man from Budapest who eternalized them in several paintings.

Rosenthal didn't last long in Parisian exile and dreamt of returning to Bucharest via Graz and Budapest in order to incite the revolution anew. In Budapest, however, he was arrested, thrown into prison and tortured to death in 1851. The idea of a bourgeois revolution was so loathed by the Habsburgs—even when it threatened an enemy state—that they made every effort to seize their own citizens fomenting rebellion in foreign countries in order to bring them home and leave them to rot in casemates like those in the Špilberk fortress in Brno. In old age, Maria Rosetti, the mother of eight children and author of the first feminist article written in Romanian, commemorated her portraitist, murdered at the age of thirty-one, with a moving epitaph.

The street named after her, Strada Maria Rosetti, is the extension of a road that leads eastward away from the central Calea Victoriei —named after her husband with whom she returned from exile in the 1850s. Aside from serving multiple times as minister, Rosetti also has a place in Romanian history as a founder of Bucharest's most significant bookshop, today an unimaginable undertaking for ministers in Romania and elsewhere. Dull, grey clouds had veiled the afternoon sun but it was still oppressively hot when I started out on my walk along the Strada Maria Rosetti, marvelling as I went at the urbane matter-of-factness or indifference with which wealth alternated with dereliction, creative intent with carelessness, excessively overdeveloped lots with inner-city wasteland. Between upper-class villas, I contemplated rundown farmhouses and the clutter of neglected kitchen gardens through their crooked gates. Adjacent to multi-storey apartment buildings designed in the 1930s by architects trained in Paris at the École des Beaux-Arts offset with cubist elements, were structures assembled thirty years ago from prefabricated components and no doubt already in a state of disrepair when their residents moved in. A glass palace had been built here two or three years ago, in which international companies had their offices; posted outside the front door and hidden behind dark sunglasses were several thugs, their bodies misshapen from hormone-induced upholstering, who would have preferred to tear me apart with their teeth than let me, a mere tourist without business aspirations, enter the sanctuary they had been detailed to guard.

113

Then came high, mould-covered walls that hid a hospital, its front entrance gate fortified with barbed wire as if it were a military barracks which no unauthorized individuals were allowed to enter, and no one allowed to leave without an exit pass. A sign on the gate informed me that the disabled, pensioners and members of the military receive a 30 per cent discount on the cost of treatment. For 50 metres, the street was freshly tarred then continued on damaged cobblestones from one pothole to another. A number of restaurants seemed newly opened and nearly all of them had a muscleman stationed in the middle of the entrance as if hired to scare off in the name of security anyone who showed the slightest intention of entering and possibly even wanting to eat or drink. I had the impression that on Strada Rosetti there were even more guards busy watching companies, restaurants and parking spots as well as construction pits in which groundwater was collecting and vacant lots that served as dumps for household garbage than was usual in this city where streets and sometimes entire neighbourhoods were occupied by private security guards.

I had been walking for some time when my way was blocked by a large sport utility vehicle parked sideways across the pavement and on the street, the cars raced by without interruption. A man in his late thirties stood next to the automobile, sunglasses pushed up onto his stiffly gelled hair, connected through an earpiece with his secretary, a business partner, the headquarters in Seattle or some galactic client. He was at pains to present a caricature of the new breed of wheeler-dealer rather than represent them and he watched indifferently as an elderly woman with swollen legs, pushing her grandchild in a stroller, blocked by his car like me, waited in vain for an opportunity to cross to the other side of the street.

At that moment, like vengeance from another world, a three-wheeled contraption lumbered up. It was too large for a handcart and too small for a haycart, recklessly assembled from any manner of wooden and metal parts—a rattling, clattering, joint-creaking monstrosity. Two men energetically pushed it along the pavement and right up to the SUV before swerving in an elegant arc out onto the street to the squeals of car brakes. A misshapen man sat enthroned upon this rickety state carriage in a makeshift jerry-rigged wheelchair: king of this street, surveying his kingdom with imperious serenity. The contraption passed us at full tilt and the fact that it was able to get so alarmingly close to this crook's car and on top of that was carrying a disabled man who gave a look of aloof disdain at the crooked businessman, who prided himself on own his aloofness, so enraged was the said businessman that he began furiously cursing the three Roma. They looked at him with concerned astonishment yet said not a word of defence or mockery. They simply looked at him, offering only their displeasure and silence as fuel to stoke his rage, such that he soon looked ridiculous with his slavering and before long began to shrink to a blustering thing, to shrink, in fact, to nearly nothing at all. He quickly took refuge in his SUV, hiding his humiliation behind its tinted windows, and roared off down Strada Rosetti.

'Kindred of kings' is how Alfred Margul-Sperber described the Roma in a great poem that ends with the lines: 'But you are ancient heralds / of the divine belief that there is but one homeland: / the world.' Margul-Sperber came from Bukovina and in his youth had himself embraced the world as his homeland. He lived in Paris, New York and Vienna, driven by the longing for 'the big city', before returning to where he had been born in 1898: to Storozhynets, 'the small Bukovinian city surrounded by red beech forests and wild peasants of which Europe knows nothing'. This man, praised by many for his readiness to help others, his polyglot esprit, his vast learning that encompassed American, Chinese and French literature, and his eloquent gregariousness, was a soul riven by agonizing contradictions. One of these never resolved and regularly resurfacing contradictions was his inability to choose between the metropolis, the wide world and the provinces, the marginal world. His first volumes of poetry alternated between expressive invocations of the 'enchantment of industries' and the big city's 'enormous body' and elegiac conjurations of the forests' rustling and villages at night. He was torn between the longing to sink into the anonymity of the metropolis and the desire to lead a life of community service in the village of Jews, Romanians, Ukrainians, Roma and Ruthenians. He dreamt of devoting himself solely to poetry free from professional obligations and yet liked to take on official positions and functions that depleted his strengths and forced him to compromise. He had a talent for these positions but at the same time he feared them. His service both garnered him recognition from the powerful and marred his reputation for a long time. He was reliable and in his legendary willingness to help others, he betrayed no one except himself.

When the Second World War began, Margul-Sperber had been in a small town called Burdujeni for several years in the surreal-sounding position of a foreign-language correspondent for an English–Romanian meat canning factory. He had withdrawn to this spot and this profession but kept writing even in complete retreat from the world. From Burdujeni, he sent brilliant articles covering all aspects of political and intellectual life of the time to be published in Bucharest and Czernowitz as well as letters to correspondents throughout the world, such as Hermann Hesse or Stefan Zweig, who knew and respected even his poems published in very small print runs. But at this point, he needed to go underground, not to survive intellectually and artistically in the provinces, far from the hustle and bustle, but to survive National Socialism; for Margul-Sperber, the most erudite and passionate champion German literature ever had in Romania, was Jewish and when the authoritarian regime of Marshal Antonescu entered into an alliance with Nazi Germany, he feared for his life. Margul-Sperber was also the most prominent translator of Romanian literature into German and that may have saved him since, with the help of German and Romanian friends, he was able survive the years of persecution to which 200,000 Jews and countless Roma fell victim.

He lived the last year of his life on this street. He was so highly regarded for his ingenious translations of Romanian folk poetry that he was awarded the Romanian State Prize, which came with many privileges, in 1954—a time when other writers were being silenced or imprisoned. Margul-Sperber could write in many registers and had the dangerous talent of composing nimble, brilliant lines, of mastering verse forms and rhymes such that he, who had spent four proletarian years in the United States as a young man, could still, in old age, translate the difficult poetry of Walt Whitman or e. e. cummings into Romanian and, conversely, bring Romanian poetry to American readers. His enormous linguistic gifts allowed him to write magnificent as well as revolting poems. He could reel off occasional poems with ease, even when he was commissioned by the Party to write one celebrating some ignoble event, a militant paean, for example, or a pathetic anniversary ode. Margul-Sperber's greatness as a poet only became clear with the posthumous editions of his works which includes poetic treasures he wrote early in his career for various expressionist journals and poems he wrote for his desk drawer while churning out politically pious eulogies.

His apartment on Strada Maria Rosetti was the gathering place for Romanian and German poets whom he tirelessly encouraged. His friend, the poet Moses Rosenkranz—who, in contrast to Margul-Sperber, was persecuted by the communist authorities—called him the 'gentle giant'. Margul-Sperber was a tall man and Oskar Pastior praised his 'mountain-like back' because he shouldered so much important baggage of the mind. 'It was not granted to me to live,' he wrote with resignation in the late poem 'Song of Sleep'. This man, who translated so many classics of Romanian literature, including the works of Tudor Arghezi, also published fourteen volumes of his own poems, countless forewords and explanatory notes as well as thousands of glosses, reviews and commentaries, seemed, as an author, as though he were hoping for death and posthumous vindi-cation and honour. A poem included by Peter Motzan in his selec-tion of Margul-Sperber's works ends with the lines: 'I have words I do not name: / One day, when I am silent, they will speak loudly.'

The apartment building in which he died, in 1967, is an inter-esting three-storey structure from the 1930s when functionalist modernism was a popular architectural style. Its grey–green facade is pierced by narrow slit-shaped windows. The building's narrowest side faces the street. With a similar building across from it and a third set far from the road, it forms a U-shaped courtyard open to the Strada Maria Rosetti. Gone are the chestnut trees with massive branches that he gazed upon during his final months when he rarely left the apartment filled with 12,000 books and many still unpub-lished manuscripts of anthologies he had spent decades compiling.

Where the chestnuts must have once stood, there now idled a white bus of the Great Romania Party, Partidul România Mare, led by Vadim Tudor, Ceauşescu's delirious court poet, who had once compared the conducător's historic mission to the eternal laws of the universe and the leader himself to a constellation and now blathered about the superiority of the Dacian race and daily proclaimed civil war on all enemies of the proud, perpetually wronged and betrayed Romanian nation. The great Romania of România Mare, which counted the unhappy childlike old woman of Văcăreşti among its adherents, will never be great enough to make room for those who had always lived here: for the Romani, the Jews, the Hungarians and certainly not for the Hungarian Jews who, like Konstantin Rosenthal, were killed because they fought for the union of the Romanian principalities, or for German Jews like Alfred Margul-Sperber who extoled the gypsies as a kindred folk.

Taurinus Olomucensis (The Neo-Latinists V)

He was called Stieröchsl, the bull, and he came from Olmütz. But he earned his fame among the learned of Europe under the name of Taurinus Olomucensis. Between Siena, Sélestat and Bucharest, Latin was the common mother tongue of those who were uprooted and selected for an education, those who had been removed from their parents' home in order to come of age in the bosom of the Roman Catholic Church, free of any bonds outside the indissoluble Church. A widely travelled man, who oversaw parishes in Moravian Brno, Silesian Legnica and Hungarian Esztergom, Stephanus Taurinus Olomucensis ultimately served as archdeacon of Transylvanian Hermannstadt. There he, who corresponded with humanists scattered across Europe, wrote the only work that has been preserved;

and there, in a country where Hungarian magnates ruled over German citizens and Romanian farmers, he died at the age of thirty-four. Five hundred and fifty years after he had written his epic poem, *Stauromachia*, in Latin, it was exhumed from the monastery library grave, translated into German and published in an apocryphal book in 1967 by a German publishing house in Romania, only to disappear again immediately before falling into my hands in an antiquarian bookshop in Bucharest. This German from Olmütz, who preached in Transylvania, and felt at home wherever his church sent him, has recorded in this book for scholars of all nationalities an account of his European adventures and a war that agitated his contemporaries and shattered their belief in the God-given order of things.

Taurinus recounts his arrival in Rome as a member of the Cardinal of Esztergom's retinue because a new crusade against the Turks was going to be proclaimed and organized. This crusade, however, did not lead to a victory of the Christian armies in the East but to a peasant revolt in the West in which both the rebels and the authorities called on God and the Bible in their murderous zeal. Taurinus' subjective and striking, if somewhat clumsy, account of his dangerous journey home by ship from Italy to the Croatian city of Senj and from there overland to Hungary is as personal and memorable a document as any author could write at a time in world history when the worth of the individual was first being recognized and personal experiences conveyed in literary forms.

Anyone planning a crusade needs not only a religion which he will defend with the sword but also soldiers who are ready to wield theirs. Where could these be found in an era when wars were so technically advanced that they could no longer be won by

Christian armies alone? Pope Leo X promised the bonded peasants of Transylvania their freedom if they would join the army of Christendom for the glory of Jesus Christ and the salvation of their souls. A hundred thousand of these *kurucs* answered the call issued by the legendary cavalry captain György Dózsa on behalf of the pope because they preferred to march on Jerusalem as God's warriors than keep toiling at home for their feudal lords. They had not gone far when they received new tidings that their Christian landlords demanded they return and if these men, who had sacrilegiously decamped in holy war, refused, then their wives and children would be forced to labour in the fields.

What then occurred made the entire continent tremble. The tremors in Transylvania that shook the old order in Europe were felt in distant lands. The tens of thousands who had set off to fight the Muslims, stopped, considered the fact that the Christian counts and barons were subjecting them to far greater suffering than the Ottomans, and swiftly marched back. At their head was György Dózsa, Georg Dosza, Dósza György, Gheorge Doza or Juraj Doza, as he was known to different nations. His shift in loyalty is puzzling since he came from noble stock and had, until then, been known as the iron fist of Christendom that beat the Turks without mercy. At this point, however, he was suddenly overcome with a raging revolutionary zeal. He didn't just want to avenge the injustice of his soldiers being promised freedom by the pope only to have it denied by the nobility or punish the magnates for narrow-mindedly pursuing their own interests, no, after a few weeks he had set eyes on a complete overthrow of the traditional order that would put the highest classes on the bottom and the lowest on top. He now wanted to break the rule of the aristocracy who feast and push God's children into poverty; eradicating this plague was the work of a good Christian for the antichrist was risen in the aristocracy and could only be vanquished through annihilation. With the military acumen for which he was renowned and with the savagery that had until then earned him praise because he had unleashed it on the godless heathen, he swept Hungary, Transylvania and Wallachia clean of the nobility; he evicted or massacred them when they refused to leave. When the pope in Rome, horrified by the effect of his bull, revoked it and commanded the soldiers of his crusade army to return to their villages since they were battling on the fields of the wealthy instead of in holy war, Dózsa and his men renounced their obedience to the pope, reviling him as a traitor to the Christian message. They led with a cross in every battle, for they believed that the papists and aristocrats were the real heretics.

The dauntless Stieröchsl's account is fittingly appalled and yet expressed in well-formed Latin hexameters. It is remarkable that he allows himself both horror and understanding. He neither praises Dózsa as a liberator of the peasants or a pious holy warrior, nor does he make common cause with the feudal lords who exacted terrible revenge and, victorious, set Hungary and Romania back hundreds of years. The enormous mercenary army that these lords had marshalled completely annihilated the peasant troops. And when the Ottomans invaded Hungary a decade later, there were no peasants left to fight them. Several thousands were dead and the authorities did not dare rearm those who had survived the severe corporal punishment that was meted out to them. As a result, the Hungarian territories whose lords wanted absolute power over their peasants fell to the Ottomans.

When the Ottomans conquered Hungary in 1526 and established a foothold in Central Europe, György Dózsa had been deaf for twelve years and the chronicler Taurinus Olomucensis for seven. After his lost battle, Dózsa was executed in Timişoara—the aristocrats, chosen by God to rule on earth, set a smouldering iron crown on his head and a scorching iron sceptre in his hand and roasted him on a heated iron throne. After paying him homage on his martyr's throne as the 'King of the Peasants' until he was completely charred, they cut his corpse into four pieces at the spot where the Marian column stands in Elisabetin, the district of Timişoara named after the Empress Sisi. I stood before this column one grey morning.

Taurinus recounted the great massacre with horror but also in a way that would show the rulers that it was their remorselessness that had provoked a rebellion such as never been seen before in Christian Europe and caused great death, destruction and religious disorder. In 1967, Bernhard Capesius who rediscovered the Latin writings of Stephan Stieröchsl from Olmütz, transposed the latter's charge into verse: 'Nefarious and indecent is poverty / Enemy of every noble custom . . .'

CHAPTER EIGHT

The Backdrop of Opole

On the fifth day of my trip through Poland, I was already so exhausted that I boarded the train leaving Krakow early in the morning with the hope that it would be endlessly delayed and take far longer to reach Opole than the scheduled three hours. The expression of the sullen conductor, who summoned the newly boarded passengers together with surly commands, as if he were the *conduttore* of a vaporetto stormed by Venetian tourists, became unexpectedly gentle when I told him of my fragile state. He soothingly promised to wake me just before Opole and gave the boisterous teenagers in the compartment a pre-emptive dressing down and ordered them to kindly show consideration for me. The train had barely shuddered its way out of the Krakow train station when he laid a hand on my shoulder and said that we were about to arrive at my destination. The compartment was empty. The docile hooligans had slipped away on tiptoe in Katowice, Bytom or Strzelce. The Polish *conduttore* hauled my bag from the luggage rack, wished me a pleasant stay in beautiful Opole, and disappeared, no doubt to do good deeds for another because in leaving the realm of his responsibilities I was no longer to be helped.

I stared in amazement at the train station. It seemed to me more like the interior of a castle, not a massive, fortified structure, but a small, playful fortress built by someone who as a child had dreamt of being a knight but grew up in a time when others boasted of becoming a famous race car driver. The deep-red structure and adorned with all kinds of ornamentation—round and square windows, turrets, oriels and gables—did not exactly make a surreal impression but gave me the feeling that there was something winningly off about it. This 'medieval castle', I later learnt was classified as a historical monument even though it was only 100 years old.

Opole is an old city that is young in every aspect but looks old in a way that it never was. Located in southern Poland, halfway between the industrial city of Katowice and Wroclaw, it was once known as Breslau, in the middle of a region that, until 1945, was called Upper Silesia. German merchants had moved to the area as early as the Middle Ages when the city and state were ruled by the House of Piast, the first historical ruling dynasty of Poland. Soon after this dynasty died out in the sixteenth century, the Habsburgs not only incorporated the city into their growing empire but also absorbed its riches into their private property. The first favour they did for Oppeln—the city's German name which remained operative for centuries—was to plunder the Piast Castle and ship the works of art and jewellery, the collections of arms and armoury and paintings to Vienna for their own treasure houses, where they are still mar-velled at today. After several wars, Silesia became a Prussian province, and the Oppeln region also remained part of Germany after the Prussian-German Empire finally collapsed in 1918, when parts of Silesia fell to the newly established Poland. The results of a plebiscite monitored by the League of Nations showed that nearly 20 per cent more inhabitants wanted their region to remain part of German than to be annexed to Poland.

About the 'Silesianness' that has been celebrated in countless songs, much has been written that is mythical and questionable and not only by nationalists of one side or the other, German or Polish, to which one could have added a third, the Czech side. No, questionable things have also been penned by those who have invoked the anodyne myth of a Silesianness that hovered between nationalities, and would invoke it again today as a supra-national Silesian identity uniting German, Polish, Czech elements as well as the spirit of the landscape into something particular, into a uniquely Silesian element...

A 1910 census asking all the Silesians of the Oppeln region about their languages revealed that the majority spoke only German, a considerable minority spoke only Polish, and only a small number of people used both languages. This small group, it was claimed, represented the 'real' Silesian and as such were later assumed to be the majority in their former homeland. As in many other cities and regions of Europe that, to everyone's benefit, were populated and shaped by various nationalities, the inhabitants in Silesia also lived more next to each other than with each other. (It is astonishing how few of the German-language writers in Prague could speak Czech, just as Czech-language writers knew little about their German-speaking colleagues. Although they all lived in the same city, they preferred to frequent the cafes where their own language was spoken and remain among themselves.)

Opole lies on both sides of the Oder River which branches into a side canal near the southern edge of the city so that the river and the canal enclose a marvellous, lovely island and the most beautiful part of the old city is on the other side of the canal. But what does 'old city' mean in this case? Opole, which is mentioned in documents as early as the thirteenth century as 'Civium Oppolensium', is a young city with a population of 130,000, almost a quarter of whom are students at the various technical colleges and universities, all founded only a few years ago.

I followed Krakowska, the street that leads from the main station straight into the city centre and transforms into a pedestrian zone after a few hundred yards. Under the midday sun, I rounded a bend—and was in Florence. Before me rose the Palazzo Vecchio with its substantial tower and its facade gleamed in the mild Polish spring light in a strikingly Florentine fashion. In the fourteenth century, the citizens of Oppeln, a confident merchant community, had built a massive town hall on their large market square. As happens, it fell victim to city fires and was repeatedly rebuilt, more magnificently each time—for the newer the times, the older a town hall the people of Oppeln wanted. In 1864, they added the tower to the town hall, which had been altered so often even in the twentieth century that the entirety was no longer sound and on 15 July 1934, the tower offered the singular spectacle of collapsing before everyone's eyes. Two years later, the Palazzo Vecchio tower was rebuilt with better static calculations but otherwise true to its 1864 prototype, which in turn was true to its Florentine model from 1320. Only then, in 1936, were the people of people of Oppeln satisfied and did not want an even older city in the future.

The town hall is enclosed in an oddly named, quadratic 'ring' of buildings, an architectural enclosure that is rarely to be found in Central Europe today. Thirty-two magnificent baroque town houses, their facades boldly painted light-pink, green, yellow, ochre, blue and orange, line the Rynek, one connected to the other, around the market square, in the centre of which presides the Palazzo Vecchio. None of the baroque town houses is more than sixty years old. During the Second World War, the 'Führer', who so loved his Silesia that he preferred to have it completely demolished than to surrender it, declared Oppeln a fortress city. In 1944, the residents were forced to vacate their city for the Wehrmacht who had been ordered not to give way before the advancing Red Army. After they fulfilled their mission, not a single building was left standing on the ring. The 170 residents who had remained in Oppeln witnessed the end of the war from a pile of rubble.

After 1945, when Oppeln had become the Polish Opole, the Germans who returned to their city and the Poles who had moved there from the eastern part of their country after it was seized by the Soviet Union, rebuilt that pile of rubble into a new city that looked older than the one that had been destroyed in the last days of the war. The ring with its baroque town houses was rebuilt more ornately in the people's democracy than it likely had ever been, because the city planners used the original building plans from the sixteenth and seventeenth centuries, rejecting any feature that had been added to the town houses at a later date. I marvelled as I crossed the baroque square of a Germany city, unblemished by even the slightest stylistic incongruity, and I found myself on a Polish city's modern main square without a single building, aside from the Palazzo Vecchio, that was more than ten years older than I was.

I had an appointment with the editor of a Silesian weekly at five o'clock in the bar of the Theatre of 13 Rows, located in one of these magnificent, new old houses on the west side of the ring. In this theatre in the 1960s, the director Jerzy Grotowski, who later emigrated to Italy, led a theatre company that was only authorized to perform for a very limited audience and yet was renowned throughout Poland. In Krakow, I had been warned that the editor would probably turn out to be a rabid proponent of Greater Germany who would try to sell me on an abstruse and twisted version of Silesian

matters. A friendly man whose face and stature were reminiscent of
Lech Wałęsa, he seemed, with his enormous moustache and beer
belly, to want to more than match the world-wide stereotypical
image of Polish men. When he attempted to order beer for both of
us it turned out that we were in an 'abstainers' bar'. As soon as the
waiter heard the word 'beer', an expression of disgust came over his
face and he pointed out that obviously they did not serve alcohol in
any form, mixed or diluted. When the alleged revanchist who
worked for the Silesian weekly wanted to begin interviewing me, it
became clear that his German was as inadequate as my Polish and so
we had to struggle through our conversation in English. We sipped
our glasses of apricot juice and when we realized that neither of us
knew the English word for this or that, we had to laugh about the
doubtfulness of any conversation held in a language which neither
party speaks fluently.

The Silesian Esperantist: Memorial Page for Jan Fethke

When the Prussian government demanded that the residents of
Oppeln declare their nationality in a 1910 language census, only a
small minority insisted that they felt equally at home in German and
in Polish and, therefore, neither could nor would choose only one
nationality. In that year, Jan Fethke, a child of both nationalities,
began his schooling. He would go on to become a German writer
and a Polish film director who was not content with having successful careers in two languages.

Even in a city like Oppeln where residents of various nationalities had lived together since time immemorial but still could not
understand each other's language, Jan Fethke and a small group of
kindred spirits came up with a solution that was as disconcerting as

it was obvious. They did not expect the Poles in the city to learn German or the Germans to master the language of their Polish neighbours. No, Fethke and his fellow enthusiasts wanted a common language spoken not only by everyone in Oppeln but by everyone around the world, a language in which every person could understand the other and their squabbling and strife would be resolved. In short, Fethke was an enthusiastic advocate of the movement based on the language invented with great linguistic creativity and political idealism by the valiant Polish doctor Ludwik Lejzer Zamenhof—Esperanto.

If the residents of Oppeln showed little interest in learning their neighbours' first language, then they would have to find common ground in a third language. The answer to the census' nationality question would be given in Esperanto in Oppeln and around the world. The so-called drawback of Esperanto—that it is an artificial language and not anyone's mother tongue—seemed to the Esperantists to be more of an advantage. From the many that he spoke or whose grammar and vocabulary he could learn from books, Ludwik Lejzer Zamenhof had assembled, in solitary hours, a new language more logically constructed than any spoken language ever was and furthermore easier to acquire than any other except, of course, for one's own mother tongue. Because Esperanto was equally strange to everyone, it would serve to connect those who had remained strangers even though they knew each other. Naturally, Zamenhof was also thinking broadly and intended for Esperanto to become the language of international understanding and large conferences and create a lively exchange between all peoples. More than the utopia of a world language, however, Esperanto was the ideal of a common European tongue, which only someone who had grown up in

Central Europe with its insoluble and conflict-prone web of language and nationalities could think of devising.

Jan Fethke began writing novels as a teenager, first in German, then from his early twenties on he wrote a series of crime novels in Esperanto under the pen name Jean Forges. The best known, *Mr Tot Aĉetas mil okulojn* (Mr Death Buys a Thousand Eyes), appeared in 1931 and became a bestseller in many languages. Thirty years after its first publication in Esperanto, a famous film director discovered the work and made it into a film with the title *The Thousand Eyes of Dr Mabuse*. Fritz Lang's adaptation of the original is very arbitrary. He significantly altered the plot and set it in the present of 1960 rather than 1931. The story of Dr Mabuse, the greatest of criminal masterminds, does seem a little Esperantist in that it borrows scenes from so many genres and takes its themes from so many myths, that it ends up being darkly eclectic just as Esperanto was optimistically eclectic because Zamenhof borrowed from Romance, Germanic and Slavic languages to create a lucid grammar and an easily acquired vocabulary.

Jan Fethke, alias Jean Forge, from Oppeln resided in Germany and in Poland; he was considered a Pole in Germany, a German in Poland. And through all the cataclysms of the twentieth century, he believed that Esperanto could finally unite humankind into one great family. Famous movies of the Weimar Republic like *Mother Krause's Journey to Happiness* or *Petersburg Nights* in which Paul Hörbiger and Theo Lingen compete to be most charming were made from his screenplays. After 1945, Jean Forge worked as a film director in Poland. He moved to West Berlin in 1960 without running afoul of the Polish authorities. On the contrary, the strangest film for which he wrote the screenplay was a co-production of the GDR and

Poland. It entered the world in two strikingly different versions. Immediately after it premiered, the rights to *The Silent Star*—a science fiction film that presents the nuclear annihilation of human civilization as a real danger in the very near future—were expropriated from the communist producers by the American film industry. The film was altered with radical cuts, changes in the chronology and, markedly, by the renaming of characters that turned a Polish aerospace engineer into a French one and a Soviet cosmonaut into an American astronaut. Still, these changes did not subvert the intention of the film. The central premise, the devastation of a civilization on Planet Venus and the threat of the same happening on Earth, is also portrayed in the version seen by Western audiences. Whereas in cinemas in the GDR, Poland, the Soviet Union and in the Eastern bloc the film's warning came from the communist engineers, scientists and cosmonauts; in the version produced by the American film studio, this message was delivered by American, British, French and Portuguese protagonists. Viewers of *The Silent Star* in East Berlin had the same fears as viewers of *First Spaceship on Venus* in West Berlin: both were afraid of a nuclear catastrophe. But in the two worlds in which the film was screened, those responsible for the catastrophe—and thus, those to be feared—were different parties.

A film that could be shown throughout the world in the language of hope—'Esperanto' is the word Zamenhof invented for hope—could not have been as easily deployed as ammunition in the Cold War. It is certainly understandable that, after all that had befallen Jean Forge from Oppeln in Upper Silesia, he did not want to abandon the hope that Esperanto represented to him.

Opole, Silesian Illusion

I had spent the night in the guest room of the Austrian Institute inside the large Wojewódzka Library on Pasieka Island. I was scheduled for a morning interview in the institute with the 'Polskie Radio Opole'; the Polish Silesian journalist spoke to me in German just as the German Silesian editor had the previous day albeit rather poorly. The Polish journalist was an attractive young woman with flaxen hair, light-blue eyes and a cross on a chain around her swan-like neck. It would not have surprised me if she had introduced herself as the daughter of a long-established German family in Opole. But she emphasized that she had not even had a German grandmother, as many prominent citizens of Oppeln did, but instead descended from peasants who had moved here from the lost eastern region of Poland after 1945. She had learned German in school and at the Austrian Institute and spoke it fluently and flawlessly with only the lightest of accents. I was pleased to recognize her accent not as the one with which Poles tended to speak German but, rather, as the Silesian accent I remembered from my childhood, having grown up in a family of so-called 'ethnic Germans'. Because my father was the director of the Refugee Advisory Office for Volksdeutsche in Salzburg, we were visited by any number of displaced people who spoke an exotic German—guttural, soft and with dark vowels—and were designated with such strange epithets as Bessarabian, Silesian or Banat Swabian.

It was almost noon when I headed to the old city across the green footbridge—called the Penny Bridge because it once charged a penny toll—wanting to escape the density of the old city for the island parks. I had learnt by then that in Opole appearances did not deceive but were reality and reality had a theatrical air to it so that the residents were always playing a role for more than thirteen rows of spectators and had perhaps long forgotten that it was a role in their own play. On the other side of the canal, I took the path lined with opulent weeping willows—named after Wolfgang Amadeus Mozart of all people. Some aspects of the often-rebuilt Cathedral of the Holy Cross still recalled its Gothic origins, but the tall, elegant neo-Gothic towers were added to the main building in 1899 which did not trouble the young priest who was my guide. Gothic is Gothic, after all, whatever the time period, he explained, for it is not an era but a spiritual approach to earthly things, an exceptional creative drive to shape matter. The way he expounded on the subject, radiant with a clergyman's pedagogical eros, left me no choice but to believe this young man with a pale face who, in the totality of his appearance, could only be described as beautiful.

A friend who had worked as a correspondent for a major Polish magazine and knows the country much better than I do, had told me that one often sees attractive, meticulously groomed women at the sides of uncouth, dishevelled and unappealing-looking men. Because he had prepared me for this on my first trip to Poland, I did, in fact, notice this phenomenon all around me, in the inns, in trams, on park benches, in shopping centres: this disparity, this imbalance was everywhere to be seen, women who, regardless of age, took care of themselves and showed to best advantage what nature had granted them in external beauty in the company of beer-bellied partners with greasy hair, in tracksuits or tasteless outfits, but for which they would resemble naked apes running through the Catholic area. At that moment, because the priest was telling me rapturously about the Cathedral of the Holy Cross and Opole's other churches, I thought of my friend's observation and for the first time, I became conscious of something that had already struck me repeatedly without my being fully aware of it: the best-looking young Polish men were not to be seen walking through their cities in jeans or fashionably cut suits but in the habits of novices, friars or junior priests, often in cheerful groups, which young women gazed at with looks very different than those they send our way, that is, not looks of regret that these men were renouncing life's joys so young, but regret that it was these young men in particular who were withdrawing forever behind monastery walls or Church rules. In Opole, too, through which many couples were strolling on that spring day, it seemed that only those men who were not handsome enough for the clergy seemed to have chosen female companionship.

The priest had so rapturously prepared me for the painting of Our Lady of Opole that I was disappointed when I stood before it. More than a metre tall and painted in the manner of a Byzantine icon, it depicts the Virgin Mary with curiously elongated fingers, holding in her arms a baby Jesus who does not look at all like a child but, rather, like a miniature adult. For all the awkward technique in this painting, a beatific light falls on Mary in her green cloak that lends the hardly individualized features of her face a poignant, celestial air. The Polish King John III Sobieski had knelt and prayed before this miracle-working icon in 1683 before he led his troops to Vienna— not to recover the treasures stolen from the Piasts by the Habsburgs but to save Vienna from the Ottomans' superior military might. The Viennese are grateful to this day, and show it by disdaining the Poles slightly less than the Turks.

That evening, as I strolled once more through the city in the certain knowledge that I was seeing it for the last time, I happened on the neighbourhood they call Venice. I knew of a few 'Little Venices' in Europe, but none were as justifiably called by this name as the one in Silesia. The wavering light in the mill canal in which the facades of the illuminated buildings were reflected was not the only thing that recalled Venice. Indeed, more than that, it was the atmosphere of a stage set, the theatrical element of Opole that made it seem that that city was caught in constant play of illusions such that old appeared new and new old, what was German seemed Polish and Polish German, renunciation appeared cheerful and cheerfulness dour, the provincial appeared urbane, the facades mysterious and the mysterious obvious. I looked over the canal, through which gondolas glided as if Grotowski had ordered them up, and felt tipsy even though I'd slaked my thirst for the second day in a row in the abstainers' bar with nothing other than fruit juice. I said to myself that the only thing missing was a pair of carnival-clad figures hurrying past and I vainly kept an eye out for them in the darkened alleys.

Schlonsaks, Wasserpolaks, Lachs: An Excursus on Confusion

Now things get a bit complicated. What I wrote about the results of the 1910 census in Upper Silesia which showed that the great majority of inhabitants of Opole identified themselves with either only the German or only the Polish language is true. However, to infer from this that such Silesians actually existed—despite the fact that the myth of them persists to this day—would be premature. Namely, the census itself distorted reality. The findings were the consequence of a grim nationality policy executed in Prussian Silesia under Bismarck. Bismarck and his men disrupted an age-old Silesian actuality which they tried to eliminate in the face of thousands of combative schoolteachers and supporters of ethnic traditions. The actuality was that since the Middle Ages many inhabitants of Silesia did not regard themselves to be either German or Polish and did not consider German or Polish their mother tongue.

The language spoken by these unreliable citizens—given that they were not fully cognizant of their nationality—was Schlonsak, pejoratively called *Wasserpolnisch*, or watered-down Polish, by the German authorities. The fact that Schlonsak was called Lachian by the Silesians who did not live in Prussia but a few kilometres south in the Austro-Hungarian Empire does not clarify the situation. I know this sounds unreasonably complicated, but I am not the one who is making the terminology unnecessarily confusing. This, rather, is part of the sad fate of the Schlonsaks, Wasserpolaks or Lachs because they themselves had never been completely aware of their history and those now trying to recall it must appeal to legends.

It is true that in the Silesian regions the population formed that numbered in the hundreds of thousands and developed a language with various dialects that blended elements of Polish, Czech, Slovak and German. This language is still spoken today. Its grammar follows Polish, its vocabulary is influenced by German and it includes elements of Czech and Slovak.

In the nineteenth century, when nationalism began to exert historical influence and was also exported to Silesia as the ideological cargo of modernization, those who identified nationally with Germans and their Polish counterparts began looking at the Silesians' age-old common language with equal contempt as an impure commingling that needed to be ethnically cleansed with draconian measures. They therefore designated this language, which was probably spoken by two or three million Silesians as Wasserpolnisch and banned it as a kind of diluted Polish from which the Germans as well as the Poles needed to be saved. And this banned Silesian language— Šlonsko godka / Schlonsak—was not even offered as an option in the 1910 linguistic national affiliation census. German and Polish were the only choices. The Schlonsaks did not feel they had their own nationality. While all those around them were discovering their nationalities, the Schlonsaks saw themselves as pre-national, as descendants of a territory that they did not consider as a borderland of one or the other national states. When they revolted, something the Silesian miners often did, their cause was freedom, not national unity. They did not want to become German or Polish; they wanted to remain Schlonsaks, to keep for themselves some of the wealth they were always digging out of the earth for others and to continue speaking their mother tongue. In a paper on linguistics, I recently found this example sentence of Schlonsak in which the German words are beautifully integrated into Polish grammar: 'Moj junge se szlecht auffiruje, ani se sztyfli nie wixowal'—Mein Junge führt sich schlecht auf, nicht einmal seine Stiefel putzt er. (My boy conducts himself poorly; he doesn't even clean his boots.)

Readers will laugh at this sentence and wonder if such a dialect —which furthermore differed from city to city—could ever have developed its own normal, so to speak, standard written language? Why not? Languages are flowing streams, not standing water, and over the course of Europe's history, countless dialects were lost whereas others became the foundations of major national languages. When Garibaldi unified Italy, no more than 10 per cent of these eventual Italians actually spoke Italian. What did they speak if not Italian? Well, Friulian and Sardinian, Greek and Sicilian, Neapolitan and Venetian; today's Standard Italian is based on a Florentine dialect of Tuscan, indeed the language of Dante and Petrarch. That large languages are formed when one of their regional dialects is declared the norm is not an unreasonable process; and that there are 50 or 60 larger languages rather than 500 or 600 smaller ones in

Europe today is in general neither good nor bad. Still, that one day there might be only five or six is not something I would hope for and don't believe I need to fear.

Schlonsak was spoken by hundreds of thousands of small farmers, miners and merchants who were expected by the nationalists on both sides to give up their impure mixed language and be ennobled by ceding their tongue to pure German or pure Polish. The nationalists, of course, believed that they were the personification of progress and held the old dialects in contempt as unmistakable signs of backwardness. The crotchety Schlonsak-speakers, enamoured of their backwardness, continued speaking their mother tongue at home, in their provincial daily lives both in the era of nationalism in the nineteenth century and in the decades of Communism when this language did not even officially exist. Today Polish linguists have classified Schlonsak as one of five historical dialects of Polish and rehabilitated it in their fashion. Since 1989, a movement spread from Opole demanding regional autonomy and the right to Schlonsak-language instruction in schools.

In closing my Polish trip, I passed once more through Opole then continued south along the Oder River for 70 or 80 kilometres to Racibórz, near the Czech border. I had been given the names of Schlonsak activists in Wrocław. I had grown so confused about Silesian matters that I wanted to hear from experts what the situation was with the Schlonsak Renaissance and Silesian regionalism.

I don't have much to say about Racibórz, called Ratibor until 1945. I was only there for an afternoon. Across from the train station entrance, on a small mound of gravel and sand, stands an old locomotive painted a glowing shade of green. It looks like it had been brought here from an oversized child's room. Apparently, it is the first locomotive that had run between Ratibor and Gliwice. On my way into the city, not far from the Church of the Assumption of the Blessed Virgin Mary, I passed the statue of the Romantic poet Joseph von Eichendorff who was born in this city almost 250 years ago. This statue does not make him look like the Catholic poet who mourned the past in Romantic verses, for which he is—certainly unfairly—praised in German literary history. The figure sitting on the pedestal was more of a trapper, a Natty Bumppo, who made his way through the Silesian forests and in Racibórz would rest a while and recover from his expeditions.

Like Opole, Racibórz has a main square called a ring, lined with buildings that were completely destroyed in 1945. And the citizens had also had the strange idea to rebuild their main square in Renaissance-style architecture. Only the Renaissance of Racibórz ended up rather less elegant than that of Opole. On closer look, there is no play with illusion here but an alienation displayed in architectural measure.

I met the Schlonsak activists in a chic tavern on the square. The Schlonsaks are a gloomy people, as the legend goes, who were put on the defensive by the modernization of the nineteenth century which formed the national states as well as secluded provincials whom history passed over. They have always had to labour for foreign rulers—for the House of Habsburg under its rotting feudal system, for the rapid industrialization of Prussia under the Hohenzollern, for the Polish Communists who raised a vast heavy industry around Katowice, Zabrze and Bytom, which in winter turned the snow black with coal soot while children were born sick in that classless society. But the activist were not gloomy, they were furious and did not look part as champions of discarded traditions. Quite the contrary, they were stylishly dressed and, with a worldly demeanour, they praised the advantages of modernization, which the hardworking Silesians advanced much more efficiently than the lazy Poles. However, all the wealth generated in Silesia, they claimed, had always flowed to others —the Austrians, the Prussians, then the communist and now the capitalist Poles.

From what I knew of the history of Silesia, I could not contradict them, but the longer I listened to them, the uneasier I felt. Their complaints were justified. Silesia, European heartland in the middle of the continent, had always been pushed to the margin and treated as a kind of inner colony expected to provide raw material. Still, the two activists did not look like exploited proletarians but like clever profiteers of societal change who were outraged that they, so competent, industrious and smart, had to pay taxes for people they considered incompetent, lazy and stupid. If we hadn't been sitting in Upper Silesia, in Racibórz, close to the Czech border, we could have been having the same discussion in Mantua, Turin or Como, in a cafe frequented by the perpetually incensed members of Lega Nord, or anywhere else in Europe where the rabid regionalists always consider themselves the truly disadvantaged, even when they are obviously among the privileged.

We took no real pleasure in each other's company; our resentments were too different for us to have become accomplices in them. And so we soon parted with friendly expressions of sympathy. How strange, I thought, I just met two Poles who didn't like either the Germans or the Poles but would most like to fabricate a Silesian nation and found a Silesian state to gain a measure of imperial immediacy so that they could negotiate directly with Brussels and avoid any detour through the government in Warsaw. Schlonsak, yes, that's what their language is called, but only their grandmas could really speak it any more.

Óndra Łysohorsky and the Lachs: An Epitaph

When I first heard of the Lachs—called *Lachen* in German, the same word as 'to laugh'—I had to laugh. I was convinced that the writer and antiquarian bookseller Max Blaeulich had invented them in a text he gave me to read in 1990.

Still, I should have known better since this trickster only fibs with the truth and you can believe him implicitly when he tells you something that sounds completely unbelievable. A compulsive reader of apocryphal writings, peculiar offprints and forgotten documents listed in antiquarians' catalogues, he would spend years tracking a work down, strangely patient in his sustained unrest, until he had it in his hand. Max had come across the Lachs in one such tract.

It was the Lachs poet Óndra Łysohorsky whom he had stumbled upon in an esoteric periodical. Max was intrigued by this poet who—although persecuted, celebrated, then again persecuted, finally tolerated or forgotten—never renounced his Lachian roots.

When Silesia became part of Prussia in the eighteenth century, the smaller part of the region remained under the Habsburgs and that area, the former Austrian Silesia, in which Poland, the Czech Republic and Slovakia would share borders later, was and is the Lachs' homeland. The Lachs dialect, like Schlonsak, evolved from a mixture of the various languages in the region, and the proportion of Czech is greater in the former and Slovakian in the latter. There is a long-running argument between Polish linguists who identify Lachs with Schlonsak and therefore label it a Polish dialect and Czech linguists who insist more emphatically on its closeness to Czech. The inhabitants of Opava, Ostrava and Cieszyn probably called it Lachs because at some point the Wallachs—nomadic herders from Wallachia in present day Romania—also settled in this Central European heartland.

In this region, where a great variety of nationalities came together, a son was born to the Goj family in the twin town of Frýdek-Místek in 1905 and was given the name Ervin. His father laboured underground in the mines and came home from his shift early in the morning covered with soot as if returning from hell. Then it was time for the boy's mother, whose melancholy songs Ervin would remember all his life, to begin her day's work as a weaver. The parents and their nine children suffered hardship but not hunger. Ervin spoke only Lachs with his family, Czech at primary school and in the secondary school in nearby Ostrava, German. He was equally at home in these three languages and was able to switch at will from one to the other in conversation or in writing. At twenty-three, when the Austro-Hungarian Empire no longer existed, this frail child of a miner and a weaver completed his doctorate at the University of Prague with a thesis on Rainer Maria Rilke.

Ervin was not just intelligent but also an intractable child whose defiance delighted his parents as long as it was not directed at them, who were worn down and wasting away from constant toil, but at the way of the world and how unjustly it was imposed on this patch of it. Ervin grew up in the shadow of the massive Lysá hora, the highest peak of the Beskids range and when he began to write poetry, he took on the name Łysohorsky instead of Goj and Óndra instead of Ervin. With his new surname, he showed himself to be a child of the Beskids, the mountain chain with forested slopes, bare cliff-faces and craggy valleys that inspired many city dwellers with the Romantic dream of wild nature and countless coal mine tunnels excavated in the eighteenth century, which, along with the steel plants added later, continue to destroy the environment to this day. With the first name of his alias, he aligned himself with the eternal ranks of the insurgents, since it is a tribute to the notorious bandit chief Ondraschek who filled the authorities with fear until they manage to eliminate him in 1715 by hiring an assassin. This brigand of the Beskids was a social rebel who took from the rich, but only, so the legend goes, to give to the poor.

For Óndra Łysohorsky, as a poet and a linguist, the rediscovery of the Lachs dialect was no homecoming to a lost Lachian idyll that never existed either in history or in his own childhood, but a social revolutionary protest that drew its power from the memory of his ancestors' suffering and losses as well as their music and language.

In 1934, he published the first book written in Lachs, the poetry collection *Spiwajuco piaść* (The Singing Fist). It contains a poem dedicated to the memory of his mother and was translated into many languages by great poets. He translated it into German himself, although he had to modify it in order to preserve the rhyme—to which he often returned despite his avant-garde experiments with language:

> *Rarely did you speak to me*
> *I only heard you sing the old songs,*
> *Lachian songs, that sound so melancholy.*

When he founded the 'Lachian Perspective' society in Ostrau / Ostrava in 1936, many artists and teachers joined ranks with him. The society's mission was to create and codify a written form of the language. Łysohorsky, for the first time, collected folk tales, proverbs, legends and the old folk songs he had heard his mother sing, but he was not a conservative regional writer who would have been content to praise the small, purportedly intact world nor did he seek refuge in dialect like someone trying spare the language from the demands of the modern age. His homeland poetry is as much a linguistic discovery—because the words must first be recreated in written form—as it is an expression of indictment, indignation and revolt.

When the National Socialists invaded Czechoslovakia in 1939 and dismantled the republic, Łysohorsky was forced to flee. He wanted to go to England, where he had friends; one of whom, W. H. Auden, was his translator. When Łysohorsky learned of Auden's death in 1973, he wrote a poetic epitaph that ends with:

He kept his word,
translating the words of a Beskids miner's son
into his brittle language
which speaks to the world in defiance of every enemy.

Łysohorsky's escape to England failed so he swerved to the Soviet Union. He was given a senior position at the university in Moscow, where he taught German, a language he had learned in school and from books. These included not only the militant works but also the finely written ones tainted by decadence, which he had devoured, enchanted by their tone of loneliness.

Stalin's political stance towards smaller nations was unique such that Łysohorsky was given the task of creating flyers in Lach that would be tossed out of Soviet planes over the Lachian settlement area. It is doubtful whether his international broadcasts on Radio Moscow, in which he called in Lach for resistance against the occupiers—but in by Czech emigrants' memoirs you can read that these broadcasts found an audience in distant London. This won Łysohorsky few friends among his Czech comrades, they suspected him of separatism, which was not at all part of his agenda. He was not striving for an independent Lachian state but for the Lachs' equality in a future socialist republic. However, when the republic was finally established, the socialist progress he had hoped for did not materialize, nor was Lach equality part of the equation as he had been promised by the Russian party cadres when he was in exile. Soon enough, in the state with the bureaucratic acronym CSSR, the Lach movement was seen as a conspiracy led by reactionary separatists who refused to accept the official stance that contamination of their territory by heavy industry demonstrated the superiority of socialist modes of production.

The most famous Lach poet's books vanished from the libraries and Lachness, robbed of its resistance and writers who believed in Lach as a not yet mature standard language rather than a sentimental dialect, declined into a government-subsidized folklore, like the countless vanquished nationalities that have been and are deprived of their authentic traditions and their future. Rediscovered in the Prague Spring, Łysohorsky was nominated for the Nobel Prize in 1969, but was forgotten again in the airless years that followed. In his bitter 'Short Testament' in 1979, ten years before his death, he forbade any tardy reconciliation:

With your silence, you made me great.
Over my coffin, please, not one word.

CHAPTER NINE

The Republic of Piazza San Francesco

The theatre director was portly and short, with a massive head from which dark, damp locks coiled into the sultry evening sky. He wore crisply pressed black trousers and a black silk shirt buttoned at the neck with it a red-and-blue embroidered waistcoat that differentiated him from his actors who were scurrying across the stage in white trousers and undershirts. Placidly watching the bustle that he was responsible for, with imperious gestures he would now spur it on or calm it down. It would flare and subside, surge and recede. There was a constant ebb and flow in the agitated tribe at his command, whom he would admonish with a barely perceptible lift of an eyebrow and, arm outstretched, would send to a distant seat or summon with a benevolent wave of his open hand.

A man in his mid-thirties, vigorous, but already experienced, still capable of impetuous outbursts and already capable of watching himself ironically during these eruptions, the theatre director held sway not only over the actors but also over the audience who crowded here in large numbers and seemed zealously eager to assume every one of the director's gestures was directed at them and to take the places he assigned them. Not that any of them would have sat down before he had calmly looked them over and finally invited them, with an amiable flash of his eyes, to take a seat. His actors might cheer or berate each other when they got in each other's way or carelessly stood in another's path, and with all their yelling, laughing and singing, they never stopped rushing offstage and, returning with a heavy load of props, running all around the auditorium. They were guided almost wordlessly by the director, the one who knew where all this movement was leading.

We had arrived in Naples at night and had a room in a hotel of threadbare respectability. Five-storeys high, it stood on the edge of the old city, on the noisy Corso Garibaldi, a few metres from where it opens out onto the ugly Piazza Garibaldi along which columns of cars drove through the entire night, cutting each other off at the exits until they were all blocked. Eventually the cars did manage to sort themselves out and drive away out of the city. On an aimless stroll, we followed an alley that branched off the Corso diagonally across from the hotel. After a few hundred metres, it brought us to a strange square. This square had a strange shape, resembling a crooked triangle, as if no building plans had been drawn up for it. No, the Piazza San Francesco is not one of Naples' attractive squares, but its apparent lack of structure concealed a beauty that only gradually revealed itself: I recognized its secret before its splendour, which overwhelmed me once I'd found it out. The obvious secret of the hidden beauty was—the theatrical element that turned spectators into actors and turned the square into a stage on which they were performing a play called 'The Square'.

A narrow street filled mostly with moped traffic cuts through the Piazza San Francesco on its longest side which measures about 50 metres. The moped riders here show off their stunts and driving more wildly than is allowed elsewhere. They ride with no hands, talking on their mobile phones all the while, zoom straight at each other, braking at the last minute and, instead of mowing down their counterpart, drape an arm around his shoulder. They gun their motors while talking with patrons sitting on plastic chairs outside the small Bar de le Torri. Flanking the bar, a cube of a building that looks as if were merely built for some makeshift purpose but has stood there forever, are slender cypresses with black tips that rise sharply towards the sky and seem to tremble convincingly even in still air. A few steps from the bar, the Porta Capuana, an imposing, free-standing fifteenth-century city gate looms over the southern end of the square. Its two towers, one named 'Onore', the other 'Virtú', call attention to the aspirations of a long-defunct sovereign; the marble arch that connects the towers dedicated to honour and virtue somehow makes this white architectural tour de force look grim.

Opposite the towers stand a few connected multi-storeyed apartment blocks, whose residents seemed to live at their windows and for the theatre. Clusters of people hung over the windowsills, men in undershirts smoking and watching the goings on below, women in curlers and robes gazing out into the evening with convincing indifference. We were an audience watching a performance—although we did not know what kind—yet we sensed that they were the real actors. Each had chosen his or her own role, some as extras, others as actors, waiting discreetly for their dramatic entrance.

Across from the Bar de le Torri, some 30 metres from Porta Capuana, we finally found the main stage. The theatre director had so graciously motioned for us to approach that we couldn't help but follow him and, after crossing the flowerpot-lined border of his realm, take our places in the loge he indicated with an excellent view of quadrangle that was the area of his immediate dominion and of the entire square of which he was the spiritual centre. 'O'Luciano' was the name of his theatre company. The stage that extended into the audience area consisted of twenty-four tables with six chairs each in the open air. On the top three stairs leading to the centre of the theatre, the director stood almost motionless and urged the nimble attendants who were rushing towards the tables—arranging or removing bottles, plates, glasses and bread baskets. Their ludicrously rapid pace was only possible because every single movement had been rehearsed. All the guests were shouting at once—they raised their empty glasses, tapped their forks on their plates as soon as they were empty and tried to catch the impresario's eye to point out the untenable situation—a chorus of many voices that proclaimed opposition and agreement in such a way that they became indistinguishable and furious protest became recognizable almost as a unique form of consent.

A hefty man clad in the troops' white had set up a stand a few steps' distance from the director where he repeated the same gesture for hours without flagging. A sieve in one hand, he scooped mussels from a vat, scattered them over a slice of toasted bread the size of a plate, which he gripped in tongs in his other hand. He then dropped the sieve, grabbed a ladle full of the stock in which the mussels had been simmering and poured it over the mussel-laden bread which he slid onto a plate and covered with a second plate before flipping it without spilling a drop. The process, repeated several hundred times over the course of the staging, took less than ten seconds and appeared to be the man's favourite pastime. He did not rush; instead, for each order, he took the necessary time, as one does for a cherished pursuit.

As swiftly as the waiters carried the plates to the tables—all the while, without glancing at or slowing their steps, they unerringly avoided the children playing on the ground and running between the tables—the guests devoured what was served them. We did not see anyone consult the menus on the tables. The waiters did not even bother taking individual orders, but simply checked that the six designated extras took their places at the table, and shortly after, brought plates of the one dish everyone wanted, along with wine, water and bread. When all the tables were full and the production played out without a hiccup, the hour of the actors and extras from the neighbouring houses had finally arrived.

From his window overhead, a thirty-year-old began to disrupt the performance—he was, as I later realized, one of the supporting characters. A gruff, raucous complaint rang from his second-storey window as he leant out gesticulating wildly. The director gave a questioning look to a short, wiry waiter who, having just lifted the tray on his right arm, called something over the heads of guests to the director in response to his silent question. The director then bowed modestly to the nameless resident and quickly calmed the latter's rage with perfunctory gestures. A minute later, the man appeared— the first of the actors who would trickle out from the apartment backdrop—accompanied by a young woman, three small children and an old woman. Her clothing and attention fixed on the children, who had been dressed up for the outing, made it immediately clear she was playing the role of the grandmother. The young man found his table that had only just been occupied and was now set for him —how exactly, we could not tell. A haughty smile played around the director's lips; his height and posture, the shape of his head, and his confident, occasionally mocking gaze was reminiscent of how Napoleon is often portrayed in films.

More and more frequently, plaintive, snide, indignant and pleading calls from the apartment blocks began to mix with the clamour of the actors and spectators already involved in the action, and as expected, nearly all the residents of the buildings flowed into the stream of the actors. Those in the preferential seating outside Bar de le Torri who did not have to yell to catch the director's attention, stayed longest. They entered the stage later and more nonchalantly than those who had entered before them and would also have to leave first. The number of guests that entered the open-air theatre was same as those left the venue—the replacement of those who were satiated with those who were still hungry occurred seamlessly. It was easy to lose oneself in contemplation of the exchange much as one does on the beach, watching the play of waves that are all the same and yet different.

In this manner, three or four teams of servers fed three or four rounds of guests at each table until midnight. We were the only ones who lingered at our places, not pressured by anyone to leave after eating our servings of the dish. We alone enjoyed the garlic-marinated mussels on flatbread that was smothered in white wine, a meal as simple as it was refined, its flavour composed of only a handful of ingredients, without being evicted from our table on finishing. It was as if the theatre director wanted us to watch the play to the very end, and as we admired the ingenuity at work, we noticed that all the spectators and actors were regarding us with increasing friendliness. Quite a few of those who were exiting the stage nodded at us approvingly, as if we had played our parts to their satisfaction.

The performance reminded us that humans hunger not only for food but also for self-expression and recognition, and this two-fold hunger need not disfigure its countenance into a grimace of greed, but can charm with artless joy. Those sitting at these tables had not only consumed a meal but had also expressed themselves through this play in which each person was connected to the others by filling their own belly. It was impossible to determine which was more important—eating or self-presentation. Indeed, I had the impression that they found each of these activities incomplete without the other. Just eating, in silence and alone, unnoticed and without participating in your neighbour's fortunes, was apparently not meant for the nation of Piazza San Francesco. Everyone here is compelled to theatrically express their presence in the life and society, even more than driving mopeds, lingering in cafes, strolling to the Porta Capuana or looking down from apartment windows, offered them this very opportunity: to experience themselves in this play at once as individuals and as part of a whole, as free and disparate citizens of this square.

The people in this anything but magnificent corner on the edge of Naples' old city, where tourists ended up only by chance, were neither rich nor poor, although they did seem to live closer to poverty than to wealth. And yet, they placed great importance not just on what they consumed but how they consumed it. In the act of eating, which in its bodily dimension is highly personal, they renewed their sense of belonging to the setting of their daily lives.

The theatre director unexpectedly came to visit our table. He gleamed with sweat from the effort of keeping the waiters moving and keeping control of the raucous bustle all the while maintaining dignified calm. After we paid the small amount he charged for the meal and the staging, he hesitated and asked, doubtful and filled with scruples, for a cigarette. After a few puffs, he wrinkled his brow and asked how long we would be staying in Naples. We told him and, after a brief moment of consideration, he said goodnight and instructed us to return the next day at 10 p.m. on the dot.

CHAPTER TEN

The Glass Sea: The Bells of Slaghenaufi

It was ten in the morning when we reached Lavarone. We rounded the last of many hairpin turns on the road that rose to an elevation of 1,100 metres, and before us, in a depression on the plateau, lay the lake. A few houses stood at the upper end, otherwise the shore was undeveloped, circled by beech and fir trees. In the summer, the fields became an elegant beach. That March was unusually warm, the thermometers already read 22°C. The lake was probably 200-metre wide and 350 long and the spring light illuminated its winter ice. We walked in short-sleeves and looked over Lake Lavarone, which was covered with a thin skin, a smooth, unwrinkled, transparent skin of ice. Underneath, it gleamed light blue and light green. I believed I could count the gravel on the lakebed.

Lavarone is not the name of a specific place but of a *comune* of small villages and hamlets separated by fields, hills and forests. Most of the hotels are in Frazione Gionghi, less than a kilometre from the lake, and in Frazione Chiesa, which is smaller but closer to the lake. Walking through Gionghi, we came upon the local library, closed at that hour, which was named after Sigmund Freud. After 1900, Freud had often vacationed in Lavarone and always stayed in Hotel du Lac. He started coming before the First World War when Lavarone still belonged to the Habsburg Monarchy and Italy began at the nearby border, in Veneto. Freud returned almost every August after Trentino and South Tyrol had become part of Italy. In the summer of 1923, he had sat in his suite in Hotel du Lac, examining his throat in a hand-mirror, but had failed to detect oral cancer. Man's remarkable gift of not seeing the obvious hindered his self-diagnosis. The hotel with its sign recalling the happy days Freud spent there was closed, as were the other hotels and inns that did not open until May. Then waves of tourists would return, first the older gentlemen, sentenced to 'wellness', taking their cure, followed by the hikers seeking proximity to the nearby mountains and finally the athletes for whom the region offers many options. But at the moment, the area seemed not only empty of tourists but also of residents. The lake sparkled below, the streets were empty and the window shutters were closed tight.

The road ended in Gionghi. A path led uphill for half an hour to the few houses of Frazione Bertoldi. From there, we didn't have far to go to reach Slaghenaufi and the solitude of the dead. There was not a sound to be heard, no, that's not right, there was a swishing: the wind blew constantly over the treetops that bordered the plateau we had reached. Behind the swaying border lay a large greenish-brown field with countless wooden crosses stuck in its soft ground. On this territory, until 1918 the border between Austro-Hungary and Italy, seven large military forts were built on the either side so that the static battle that was to last for years.

A hundred thousand Austrian and Italian soldiers lost their lives on the plateaus of Folgaria, Lavarone and Luserna, firing heavy artillery at each other from cliffs and forts that were only a few hundred metres apart. Nearly 1,000 soldiers of the Austro-Hungarian army are buried in the military cemetery of Slaghenaufi, which has a marvellous view of the landscape. The crosses stand in rank and file, but the cemetery has nothing martial about it. Most of the graves bear a name on a simple plate and for the first time in my life, I appreciated the work done by the War Graves Commission here—they were allowed to tend to one of the warring parties in former enemy territory and while they did not award the glory of heroes to 998 of the men mutilated and maimed in Slaghenaufi, the commission has returned to them the dignity of their own names. The bones of Szabo, Unterkofler, Giulic, Olensa, Petrescu, Divaniuk and Stefanović lie reconciled, side by side.

Around two o'clock, we were back down at the lake over which the mortars and grenades had flown, where Freud had walked along the shore towards his years of suffering; today, it lures vacationers from around the world to innocent pastimes. I stood on the shore, recalling the Ukrainian, Hungarian, Polish, Croatian and German names I had deciphered on the crosses and trying to remember the letters Freud wrote in Hotel du Lac informing worried students of his good health. The ice covered the entire lake, crumbling only at the edges, a paper-thin platter on which the sparkling sun was served at noon and which a single stone thrown from shore would have shattered. Under the glassy layer, the bells that hung in the chapel of Slaghenaufi began to ring.

The Chronicler of Patmos

We had been on the island for three weeks and the Meltemi, the northerly winds, which have so many sounds at their command— the rumble of the sea that reached us over the mountains, the whistling it makes as it rushes down from the mountain, its sighs among the branches in the garden, its mournful whispers in the olive grove, the peculiar swishing it makes as it sweeps over the arid fields, the clank and clatter of metal buckets blown over and rolling down the streets, the banging of doors and shutters in the painter's house where we were staying—the Meltemi had not subsided a single day. In the morning, my wife and daughter had driven to the beach 8 kilometres away on the other side of the mountain. I had stayed in the upper part of the white city. I was sitting on the veranda, looking out over the burnt fields in the valley, when I noticed something was missing. It took some time until I became aware of the silence as the absence of the resounding wind that I had heard day and night, even in my sleep, which no one who lives here can avoid.

The silence was so loud that I could not bear it and set out, walking through the narrow lanes glistening in the sunlight up to the small square. It was Sunday afternoon, and the city was desolate. The tourists were at the beach, the locals had retreated to their shuttered homes. The lane wound in switchbacks between the forbidding, windowless street-facing walls of the houses and I noticed that the walk was gradually becoming difficult. I stopped midway to catch my breath under a scrap of shade thrown by some protruding masonry. I could hear the Meltemi roaring inside me: it thundered in my head which had begun to throb with a sudden ache caused by the uphill walk; it billowed and sagged in my chest, which rose with each shallow breath; it rushed in my veins as blood flowed painfully from my fingertips to my toes. I hoped that somewhere in the distance a dog would bark and rend the oppressive silence or that a radio, switched on by an invisible resident of one of the houses would free me from the paralysis with loud music or incomprehensible foreign words. But the silence remained and the only thing I heard was myself.

When the rushing and roaring subsided, I walked more slowly up the whitewashed stairs that led the lane uphill for 50 to 60 metres. A few scrawny, mottled cats were dozing, stretched out on the steps. Usually so skittish that they leapt away whenever anyone drew near, they simply watched me, their yellow eyes filled with lethargic fear, as a I stepped over them, as if they would rather die than flee to a safer distance. At noontime, thoughts of escape disappear, even the self-preservation instinct is extinguished.

The closer I came to the top, the more space there was between the houses. In certain places, I could see the blue sea with its calmly rocking waves which had lost the white caps of the previous weeks. Up here it was always windy and cooler than in the maze of streets below and the heat hit me harder, almost automatically, my pace matched my heartbeat. In this state I reached my destination, the charming little square on the plateau, to which four lanes led and which was always lively in the evening since people enjoyed sitting in the cafe on the one side or in the restaurant on the other. The white walls glowed so brightly that I had to shut my eyes, and when I opened them again, the buildings around me seemed to sway in the shimmering light.

After a while, I sensed that I was not alone. In the shadow of a parapet, sat the old man whom I had encountered several times already in the upper part of the city. He was seated on the small stairs on which a few elderly people often perched in the evenings and amused themselves by watching the foreigners, as both tourists and newcomers were always called by the inhabitants, even when the latter were Greek and had lived here for years. With one leg pulled in and the other stretched out before him, he held the stick he always used on his leisurely walks propped against the pavement two steps below him. One hand was wrapped around the pommel, the other played with the string of cheap beads with which many of the island's men toyed when they were doing nothing but waiting, and waiting for nothing, or at most for time to pass, for noon to come, for the ferry to dock, for twilight to arrive, for the sun to set, for night to fall.

From the first day, I was fascinated by these bead-fingerers who were outside the realm of time, who sat impassively on steps in the city and in cafes in front of long-drained espresso cups, who stood around without bothering to find a reason or an excuse they could offer for their idleness, all the while incessantly sliding a rope of stone, glass, silver or wooden beads over the backs of their hands or letting it slip through their palms, over and over. Some were virtuosos who followed a secret and complicated set of rules that required a particular cycle for the beads and a strictly ordered sequence in the way they related to each other. There were also the careless ones who grabbed the end of their worry beads and whipped the rope back and forth around their fists. And, of course, there were the ones who believed in magic and squeezed each bead individually between thumb and forefinger to confirm its magical power, or they squeezed every second or fifth one according to the secret order with which they hope to ward off small misfortunes and great calamities.

The old man sat motionless except for the constant play of his left hand with the beads and the thought of how many hundreds of times they had slipped through his fingers already that day filled me with a terrifying sense of emptiness, a feeling of eternity stretching out in monotonous repetition from which there is no escape. The click of the beads hitting each other and the grating of those rubbing against each other were the only sounds I could hear until I noticed that I was still panting.

The old man wore brown trousers and a dark-blue, long-sleeved shirt. He sat there, lost in the play of his worry beads. The island's many idlers, all those who were waiting, waiting for nothing, who were only focused on watching time pass and could endure this delinquency were for me, coming from a world in which everyone had to be busy with something, the greatest provocation of my weeks on the island. Occasionally, when sitting in a cafe where you could linger without even ordering anything, the slowness with which everything occurred would exhaust me and, almost bursting with unexpected irritation at the boredom which represented the highest art of living here, I would be tempted to get up, grab one of the idler's ropes and berate him: Don't you have anything to do other than kill time?

Then again, after watching one of them long enough in his activity devoted to the patient wasting of time, the cud-chewing of monotony, I would begin to see myself as miserable and deformed, caught as I was in the compulsion to always be busy with something, even if that something was the concentrated observation of those who were free of that very compulsion. I would then feel like someone who was incapable of living without the constant search for distraction and amusement.

Everything I had accomplished in my life seemed to be under the curse of distraction, to be nothing more than evasions, the result of my hopeless inability to sit around like these men, to wait for nothing, to live free of any sense of obligation to do something meaningful, useful or important. Depending on my state of mind on this island—whether I was ready to follow its rhythm or wanted to resist it—these men who were completely one with their idleness struck me as idiots or sages. How else did the men in my world differ from each other than in their different activities and the different levels of accomplishment? How could the women of the island tell their husbands apart since they all did the same thing, namely, nothing?

The old man had long been aware of me and had given me time. After ten minutes, half an hour, two months, he turned his eyes away from the wall that was covered with purple and red bougainvillea and onto me, with calm interest. When I crossed the 15-metre-wide square, he shifted to the side slightly, inviting me to sit down next to him. Then we sat there together in silence.

I wonder if the old man was thinking the same thing I was, namely, that he was sitting here silently next to a stranger wondering if it was proper to simply sit there without paying any attention or saying anything to each other. But did he think, did any of these idiots and wisemen think at all? Finally, he turned and looked at me with yellow cat eyes. His face was tanned a dark brown and deeply lined with wrinkles. He wore a ridiculous red baseball cap with the Texas Riders logo. The artist who for twenty-five years had spent spring and autumn on this island and in Austria painted, transformed and reconstituted, what he had seen on the island, had told me that many Patmians must go elsewhere to find work. Even 100 years ago, more descendants from Patmos lived in Texas than on the island itself, but most people returned in their old age and said they had only endured being abroad because they knew that one day they would sit at the port again—and watch others sail away on the ferry.

In a hoarse voice, the old man started to speak, looking at me inquiringly every few sentences to make sure I was following him. I didn't understand a single word, but to keep him going, I responded with a questioning *né* or an uncertain *ochi* whenever he hesitated. What I've learned from travelling through many countries is that a yes or no in the right tone of voice will encourage almost every speaker to keep talking. And in fact, the old man kept up his lively patter in his language, of which I had trouble learning even the most basic elements. Now and then he would laugh or shake his head while speaking and wait until I enticed him to continue his tale with a yes or a no.

Once my *né* did not seem to satisfy him, so I tried a questioning *ochi* and finally a downright dramatic one. This seemed enough for him because he kept talking but a faint suspicion had been aroused and he paused more frequently. Then I heard myself speaking, telling him in my own language that after only a few days I had succumbed to the island illness, the bodily fear of not being able to leave and the painful awareness of time sluggishly trickling away. And that after a week my wife had suggested that next time I should bring my laptop in order to work a few hours each day, otherwise my sullen mood would spoil our holiday.

To distract myself from the fact that there was almost nothing to distract me, she later gave me one of those strings of worry beads with twenty-two polished, mahogany-brown stone beads and three silver beads. I willingly endeavoured to discover in them the meaning of life and to imitate all those idlers fingering their beads while they waited for nothing, but after a few hours I tossed them angrily aside, enraged at the impertinence of squandering my time at more than fifty years of age and completely exasperated with myself and my incapacity and impatience.

This is what I relayed to my companion and in my fevered confession, I failed to notice at first that as soon as I paused, he would interrupt me with an inquiring *né* or prompt me to continue with an incredulous *ochi*. But even when I realized that he had shamelessly adopted my method, I didn't care. So we sat there together, the old man who had perhaps led a life of hard work in America and I who found a life without work on this island such a torment. He would speak a little, then I would, he would ask *né*, then I would ask *ochi*; neither of us understood each other. In this way we enjoyed each other's company for a good while.

The Watchwoman of Čara

The sun was about to set behind the imposing mountain ridge overgrown with genista, Aleppo pines, firs and cypresses and from the snow-white Sveti Petar Church came the prayers of the rosary hummed by a few elderly women. It was the last Sunday in August and still so hot that we were out of breath after only a few metres uphill, so we put off the climb to the village for later. Čara lies on the one road that crosses the island from west to east and divides the island in half lengthwise: on one side of the road, lanes and flights of stairs lead 200 or 300 metres uphill, on the other, the village descends just as steeply downhill. There vineyards surround a stony quadrangle. As shadows crept over the row of houses in the upper village, the cemetery in the middle of the vineyards began to glow in the evening light.

We walked down towards the plain, past the masonry of abandoned buildings, past fig trees protruding from collapsed roofs, past bushes with bright red and purple flowers growing from between the stones. A plaque had been mounted to the right of the cemetery gate in commemoration of the Fascists' massacre of young villagers on 6 July 1943. At the time, Korčula had been occupied for three years and Italy had annexed Dalmatia. Resistance began on the day when the first boats unloaded the occupiers, guardsmen in black shirts.

The island is not large, barely 40 kilometres in length and less than 10 wide. When the carabinieri and the hated Blackshirts landed in 1941, the island population numbered little more than 10,000. Hundreds of young men and women left their families, their farms, fishing huts and workshops for the forests, described since the ancient historians as impenetrable and today still filled with thorny maquis. 'Going into the bush' simply meant joining the Partisans. Almost every family in Čara lost someone in the fight against the occupier, killed in battle, executed or shot as a hostage.

The cemetery may have glowed in the evening light on 6 July 1943 as it did on our visit. The warm mistral would have blown over the vineyards and behind the mountain ridge, the sea and sky would have been blurred as always. It's said that 100 years ago, an altar of alabaster washed up on the coast that was not visible but could be sensed. In the cemetery's small church, we admired the naive charm of the altar, a late Gothic piece that art historians attribute to an atelier in Nottingham, England, although they cannot explain more plausibly than the legend does how it could have ended up in the centre of this Dalmatian island. We noticed that aside from the loud buzzing of the cicadas, there was complete silence around us. Here, of all places, where fading letters commemorated the sons and daughters of the village who had been led into the fields and mown down on a summer day in 1943, we were tempted to escape into an image of peace. Here, of all places, we had the impression—on this island, in Čara, at this cemetery—that we were not in history so much as in eternity.

After an hour we were back on the main road; in the Sveti Petar Church, the continual singsong still invoked the intercession of the Holy Virgin. On the church square stood, sombre and gnarled, the oldest cypress of the island which had grown more in width than in height since the time when Napoleon's troops had advanced this far and forcibly imposed French freedom on the island's inhabitants. A shaggy mutt that had been dozing in the dust rose as we cautiously climbed past and looked at us in surprise as we continued on the path to the upper part of the village. Here the houses were built scenically into a mountainside that is so steep you could step from the entrance of one house onto the roof of the next. Many of the buildings had crumbled into piles of stone, from which all manner of shrubbery fought to reach the light. Still, between the stone piles, stood well-maintained, freshly whitewashed houses and flowerpots were carefully arranged along dry masonry walls that hid large inner courtyards.

In the brochure, I read that 762 people live in Čara, but we did not meet a single one of them that Sunday. I had glimpsed the backs of six or seven old women in the church who had not found a way out of their litany's endless loop and heard their exhausted murmur. In front of one house in the upper village, I thought I heard the sound of objects being moved but could see nothing through the curtains in the open window.

We had reached the upper row of houses, almost all of which were empty. A wall towered high above us, behind which the top floor and roof of a fortress-like house could be seen. It must have had a view over the village, the cemetery, the vineyards and ridge, all the way to the sea. A woman dressed in black with a black kerchief covering her head and shoulders, black tights and grey slippers made of some coarse material sat motionless, her back against a small partition wall, her legs stretched out in front of her on the wall like a young girl and her hands clasped in her lap. She had watched us stroll down to the cemetery, then climb up here. We were the only thing moving in Čara, four dots moving through the landscape at first, now four strangers who made so bold as to ascend to her proximity.

Her eyes, drilling into my back, made me pause, look back and finally notice her seated right above us. She looked at us, unmoved, and did not return my nod or my tentative greeting. She looked at me impassively, looked right through me, then turned her gaze over the village and cemetery, vineyards and hill, to where the ships came from. Below her eagle eyes, she had a finely chiselled nose. Her thin-lipped mouth was slightly open, her body powerful and compact. She was old, as ancient as the wall, maybe 90, maybe 220, maybe older. She had sat there when the altar carved in Nottingham washed up onshore, when Napoleon's soldiers brought a freedom that the islanders suffered as coercion, when the Italian Fascists autocratically annexed the island to their dear fatherland and, after they left a trail of blood, were forced to flee precipitously by the island's inhabitants.

She kept watch for the ships which had brought the Greeks, the Romans, the Venetians, the French, the British, the Russians and the Austrians, who had subdued the island for centuries or only a few years and, finally, brought the Italians. She kept watch to see which conqueror would appear on the horizon and whether writers would follow the soldiers. She lost interest in us; she stayed at her post without letting herself be distracted by the four strangers who had ventured up to her, the watchwoman of Čara.

The Old Woman of Ordu Caddesi

I saw her on the very first evening I was in Istanbul and on the following days, I always walked down the Ordu Caddesi at eleven at night to see if she would pass by again. The Ordu Caddesi is an arrow-straight road that leads from Laleli district with its tangle of streets going uphill and down where my hotel was and continued several kilometres to the magnificent, historic district between the Blue Mosque and the Hagia Sofia. Ordu Caddesi is a multi-lane boulevard in Laleli, filled day and night with roaring traffic that is hard to cross. Further on, where it leads past the massive Beyazit Mosque with its flocks of pigeons circling overhead, its name first changes to Yeniçeriler Caddesi and then finally to Divan Yolu after the Grand Bazaar, where it is reserved for trams and pedestrians.

It was there that I saw her, near the Istanbul University tram stop on Ordu Caddesi and an intersection with another main road that leads drivers off to left and right so that the boulevard won't be blocked by thousands of cars near the famous monuments. It was impossible to say how old the woman was, maybe sixty, maybe over eighty. Her body was cloaked from head to toe in a stained black sack that may once have served as a religious garment but now functioned more as rustic working garb. Her head was also covered with a black hat—not one of the fashionable head scarves that some women in Istanbul wear but a woollen hat pulled down over her ears and forehead. She was not much more than a metre tall, although her body would no doubt have been of a normal stature if she had stood upright rather than bent nearly perpendicular at the waist. In this posture, she shuffled down the Caddesi everyday at the time when the muezzin's tinny voices rang out from various directions, calling for the night's rest, or she turned from one of the side streets onto the boulevard. The shuffling sound she made did not come from her being unable to lift her feet either because she was too tired so late in the evening or because some disability made her drag her feet. It came, instead, from another source: the strange snake she dragged behind her.

It consisted of twenty or thirty plastic sacks filled to bursting that she had tied together with a rope to form a snake at least 5-metre-long that followed behind her in the dust of the street. She had fastened the rope around her upper torso to leave her hands free and, with her upper body parallel to the ground and arms swinging, she advanced laboriously with her odd cargo. She struggled along, as if deep in thought, and when she crossed Ordu Caddesi, an athletic challenge even for the young and nimble, she did not seem to pay the slightest heed to the traffic.

It was utterly inconceivable for me to speak to this woman. In the cafe at the intersection, where I drank my evening cup of that sweet tea and where the waiters already greeted me courteously like a regular, I asked the portly owner who she might be. He, who also watched her attentively every evening as she crossed the street with her arms swinging and tugging her plastic-bag snake behind, answered with something that sounded like 'old woman from the countryside'. From his tone of disgust—in reaction more to my interest than to the person I expressed interest in—his answer could just as well have been 'mutt from the suburbs'.

I never found out how the old woman earned her living, whether she suffered from of untreated Morbus Bechterew which causes painful stiffening of the spine, or if she had a congenital condition that prevented her from standing upright and gazing into the distance. She paid little attention to passers-by and seemed so absent that she could hardly be a beggar. Maybe what she dragged in the plastic bags were not personal belongings so that she could spend the night in a neighbourhood hovel, but were wares she had plied in one of the countless city markets and was now bringing home after several hours of walking.

I had already left Istanbul when it occurred to me that I had not seen her face. I had only seen her body bent at a right angle, the black bag she wore and the snake, which was so striking that I can still picture it today and how she, so far removed from the metropolis in her thoughts, dragged it through the metropolis. And I can hear the swishing sound of her snake sliding over the ground, that in my memory so drowns out the infernal noise of the cars and motorcycles, the shouts of people out on the streets until late at night and the calls of the muezzins from nearby minarets and that to me represents the sound of Istanbul.

An Encounter in the Cathedral

It was in Tours, that old city on the Loire. We had taken a detour to see the Cathedral Saint-Gatien, an imposing basilica built between the thirteenth and sixteenth centuries. It is famous for its stained-glass windows which almost completely fill the walls of the nave. Those who have the time and a knowledgeable companion can spend hours identifying figures whose stories are told in Bible. But even specialized and detailed knowledge of the figuration and the historical and biblical background could not surpass the impression made by the sun and the glass alone. On that overcast day, the sun repeatedly broke through the clouds and submerged the gloomy church in an unearthly light that changed moment by moment from blue to red to green.

We had sat, silent and amazed, for some time when I became aware of a shuffling noise. A few minutes earlier, a tour group of older men and women, all wearing shorts and tennis shoes and equipped with cameras, had been led past us towards the altar. I listened, trying to determine what the sound was. It seemed to be coming from one of the side altars a few metres to our left. I rose and followed the shuffling sound. Behind one of the massive, towering columns I saw a small chapel that was much darker than the nave onto which it opened. In the flickering light of a couple of candles sat a woman of about eighty, with her bare knees pressed together at a slight angle and perched on the edge of the pew as if she hardly dared sit on it. She was a diminutive woman who had slipped away from the group unnoticed.

The noise was caused by her exhausted attempts to eat an enormous sandwich. It was one of those baguettes with filling offered in bakeries all over France. A slice of cheese and a slice of tomato on a green lettuce leaf, as well as thin rings of onion, capers and pieces of tuna slathered with a creamy sauce are squeezed between the two halves of the long, slender loaf. I had already tried one and knew how delicious they could be. With each bite the famished woman had to struggle with drips of the creamy sauce that seeped sideways out of the baguette and trickled down the corners of her mouth. Her tongue made a wiping noise as she attempted to lick the dribble. The fundamentalist emotion that had flooded me when the tour group walked past and had me scouting around for a severe sexton who could immediately usher any shorts-clad, cud-chewing picture taker, regardless of age, out of the church immediately drained away. The slurper's desperate eyes met mine when she noticed my presence; it was the look of chased creature tracked down in a hiding place it thought was safe. No less ashamed than if I had caught her relieving herself, the elderly woman looked at me in unspeakable horror and what bound us was our shame at having encountered each other here.

Later, after she had rejoined her group, I saw her laboriously kneel before leaving the church. So she was pious, then, unlike me and I instinctively had to ask myself what I had never wondered about before: What is so bad about someone sating their hunger in God's house?

Four Grimaces with Cat

The moderately sized painting is displayed in a corridor as if it weren't fit to hang with the thousands of paintings in the large and small rooms of the museum. It seemed to have been hung apart so that it would remain unnoticed and so that visitors crossing from the room displaying local archaeological finds to the room with Gothic sculptures would pass without noticing it. And yet, I would have come to the city of Angers at the confluence of the Maine and the Loire just to see this picture—not mentioned in a single art or travel guide to the region, mind you—had I known I could find it here.

The painting is of two men, two women—and a cat. The men and women seem to be on familiar terms. All four are of noble status; their clothes, as far as one can tell from the bust portraits, are of an elegant cut and expensive cloth. What strikes the viewer at first, then prompts them to laugh before leaving them perturbed, is that all four are grinning so widely, their teeth aggressively bared, that they have a violent, frightening air. Indeed, they seem to consist of nothing but their grins. Evidently they have a secret, and they are laughing because we don't know what it is.

It must be a sordid secret—or so the white cat, stretched languidly out before them makes you think oddly enough. For the creature makes a profoundly sensual impression; you might think the cat is recovering in advance from the libidinal activities in which the men and women are about to indulge or that it witnessed goings on that were surely a breach of convention. Without the white cat, the painting would be a less witty composition than it is, and it would lack the cryptic element that makes the painting more than an eccentric game with aristocratic grimacers. The animal embodies the suspicion that the four figures are in a scandalous relationship and are as delighted about the relationship as they are about the fact that we don't know what's scandalous about it.

The cat knows more than we do and that is what gives us pause: we are not fascinated by the nasty and arrogant grins but by the question of what preceded or will succeed the scene. The picture is a work by the Florentine painter Niccolò Frangipane, about whom I could find little more information in a biographical encyclopedia of visual arts that I consulted a few weeks later on my return home than that he was born in 1555 and died in 1600. The painting's title is so literal as to seem sarcastic: 'Quatre têtes riants et un chat' (Four people laughing and a cat). If it was a commission, as most works were at the time, and the four cunning subjects were the commissioners: What instructions did they give the painter?

In the evening, sitting at one of the small tables outside the restaurant in Rue Saint Laud, which is teeming with people strolling, my attention was caught by two elderly ladies eating dinner and sharing a bottle of red wine. The faded elegance of their clothing seemed out of place here, among people wearing the very latest fashions that were on the cusp of wilting, but perhaps it was precisely because of that dated elegance that no one took any notice of them. Even I'd only noticed them after they had been discussing us for a good while. There was no doubt that they were talking about my wife and me, repeatedly giving us mocking glances, and when one of them again made a remark to the other, the latter would look at us brazenly as if she wanted to confirm with her eyes what her ears had just heard.

It's not as if I would have wanted to fetch the cat crouching by the wall on the other side of the street and place it on their table, asking: 'Where are your two gentlemen?' Yet I remembered that we had been awoken by the sound of hammering at eight that morning. We were staying in the apartment of a friend, an Austrian with whom our homeland had not been particularly kind. He had lent it to us for two weeks. The apartment was on the quiet Rue Franklin, a few minutes from the city centre. When I stumbled to the window half-asleep, I saw that although the apartment faced a respectable street, its other end opened onto a muddle of small gardens, rickety garages and sheds. Right below us, no more than 3 metres from our bed-room, two young workers from Maghreb were standing on a garage hammering a new metal roof in place. When they saw my tousled head, they traded a few joking words without even nodding at me. They did not, in the slightest, resemble the aristocrats in the painting I hadn't yet seen at that point. Instead, they were workers taking harmless pleasure in waking a lazy bourgeois with their labour. Nor could I make any connection between them and the two women who had talked about us almost provocatively and continued even after we caught them.

But it was the fifteenth-century painting that opened my eyes to my predicament in the twenty-first century. We are what others find amusing, but I keep forgetting this. And the puzzle they pose for me is based on the fact that I am no puzzle to them. They peruse my face, but what they read is something I can never hear.

CHAPTER ELEVEN

The Vandals of Fontevraud

Civic progress reached Fontevraud when the richest monastery in France was turned into a prison. The last nuns had abandoned the 800-year-old abbey in 1792. On 30 January 1793, the monastery— a small city unto itself—was ransacked and plundered. Ten years later, Napoleon ordered the entire monastery complex to be turned into a central prison. Intermediate floors were installed in the abbey church, a marvel of light with its squat nave and its soaring transept and choir. The Gothic annexes were turned into warehouses, silos and workshop, the chapter house became a storage depot, and an outbuilding was refashioned into a courtroom where offences within the prison were severely adjudicated.

Fontevraud was founded in 1101 by the charismatic itinerant preacher Robert d'Arbrissel as a holy site in his effort to restore Christian monastery life. Monks and nuns dedicated their lives to their own salvation and that of all of Christendom, serving the sick and the poor and proclaiming the good news of the Lord. Out of d'Arbrissel's workshop of humility would grow the richest monastery of France with countless branches and lucrative latifundia in France, England and Spain. All that endured of d'Arbrissel's founding principles was that monks and nuns of Fontevraud lived together, as if their chastity were only sanctified by constant temptation and that, until its dissolution, the abbey was presided over exclusively by abbesses, women from the richest aristocratic dynasties of the time, many of them daughters of kings, first the Plantagenêts, then the Bourbons.

Even in its early years, Fontevraud consisted of four priories: Saint-Jean-de l'Habit, where the monks were housed, humbly enjoying the affront of constant female domination; the Grand-Moûtier cloister, where women who had withdrawn to the convent lived in a virtuous state of virginity; the Sainte-Marie-Madeline for lay sisters, worldly-wise women who only became nuns after they were widowed or had escaped the bondage of matrimony for a life of withdrawal in the nunnery that was both free and regimented, who had, as an ancient source unequivocally tells us 'chafed enough under both husband and the world'. These nuns, who understood what they were renouncing and, to a certain extent, chose chastity from experience, were recruited from their ranks and were Robert d'Arbrissel's favourites. For centuries, they were the formative figures of this prospering convent, which also became an international commercial enterprise—a unique communal experiment and a continuously evolving Gesamtkunstwerk. The fourth priory, Saint-Lazare, was built outside the perimeter walls as a leper house that later became a care home for convalescent nuns and a hospice for the elderly in the eternal cycle of years.

I sat in the elegant courtyard of the Saint-Lazare priory, drinking tea as seemed appropriate in the afternoon, surrounded by ailing old people as might have lived here in times long past. Today's elderly are wealthy French and English visitors staying in the luxury hotel housed the same complex, since the era of progress that turned a reactionary monastery into a prison of the republic ended forty years ago. The luxury hotel has a brasserie, a pub, a cafe and a restaurant. Various elements of the old building remain: the Romanesque rooms; an elegant, winding staircase from the seventeenth century; the chapter house. On the way to the toilets, the staircase was thronged with a hobbling crowd. The English ladies leaned on the banister, on each other or on the Asian nurses they had brought with them. I joined in the slow procession, which was not held in service of heavenly worship but for the relief of earthly distress.

In the garden, two elderly French men sat at the table next to mine, sharing a dogged silence in their fraternity. The younger one, in his early seventies, smoked cigarillos with his tea; the older was bulkier but unmistakably of the same build, with the same sharp profile. His left eyelid drooped over a watery, clouded eye. He lifted his cup shakily to his lips. He seemed anxious when he glanced around or up to the row of windows where his suite was. When he slowly trudged over the white gravel to the hotel, he kept his arm linked with that of his sturdier brother. The Hostellerie du Prieuré Saint-Lazare is not a retirement home for the wealthy seeking to withdraw from the world they have chafed against to a monastery built for the poor, later overtaken by the high aristocracy and transformed into the most modern penitentiary of its time. Instead, it is a hostel for well-heeled travellers who, perhaps incautiously, embarked on a late tour through France or a final trip to the châteaux of the Loire. Many of them already seemed to regret exposing themselves—despite their waning strength—to the supposed comforts of lavish buses, high-end accommodations and expert guides, which they now experience more as hardships.

For more than 150 years, Fontevraud was a prison that held as many as 1,800 inmates, many of whom ended their lives there and others waited to be deported to a penal colony or led to the gallows. The thief and writer Jean Genet was imprisoned in Fontevraud for a few months. Enamoured with the cult of evil and worship of humiliation, he describes Fontevraud in his novel *Miracle of the Rose*, as the pantheon of French prisons—a radiant hell where only the most damned of the damned had the privilege to be thrown. After 1940, the French collaborationist regime incarcerated their political opponents in Fontevraud and in 1945, the sleezy henchmen and well-born strategists of the collaboration themselves took their place in its communal cells. The prison was shut in 1963 and most the inmates were relocated. Only forty of them remained in the Madeleine Convent, and for the next twenty years, their sole task was to eliminate all traces of the previous 159 years when the abbey had served as an enormous prison. Under the direction of the best architects and monument conservationists, they had to restore the monastic chambers, dismantle the watchtowers, remove the intermediate floors and demolish the workshops that had been set up in the formerly clerical rooms to turn the abbey into a museum of spirituality. When they had finished, the last of the inmates too were released.

The double vandalism of eliminating the culture of memory by first erasing the traces of the monastery inside the prison and then erasing all traces of the disbanded prison itself had ultimately created a space in which destruction and remembrance are united: a museum. There is no doubt that Fontevraud received the magnificent recognition that is due such a unique project, with a revivalist preacher like Robert d'Arbrissel, scores of kings' daughters, the republican Emperor Napoleon and, over the years, a few hundred thousand monks, nuns and criminals all playing their part.

I was standing in the upper dormitory, one of the three sleeping rooms in the Grand-Moûtier, which the official leaflet said was not accessible to the public, but I had found it open and was admiring the magnificent vaulted roof timbers shaped like an upturned wooden ship's hull. At some point, the old man who had had tea with his brother in the priory garden then shuffled into the hotel appeared next to me. This Frenchman was actually Belgian, I learned, and despite how tentative he had looked before, leaning on his brother for support, he now seemed composed and confident in this room, which can only be reached via a long staircase and could induce vertigo. At first I thought he wanted to explain what was obvious and immediately evident even to me, who had never aspired to be more than an awe-struck layman in architectural matters, namely, that in this dormitory the roof arching above us was like the hull of a ship. Standing beneath it inevitably makes you feel cramped, however spacious the room, because when you see the belly of a ship above, it feels like being pressed underwater with little hope of making your way to the light and the open air.

But the old man with his half-closed, watery eye had something else in mind. He told me how he had gone to sea earlier, not as a seaman or a captain but in a sailboat—which I could only picture as a yacht—and only then did I notice that embroidered on his navy blazer was the badge of a maritime association, no doubt one so distinguished that he tried to represent it with poise in a foreign country. He had probably suffered a stroke because his speech was slurred, but was delighted to have found someone to talk to. His right eye twinkled when he described a magnificent sailboat on which he had crossed who knows which body of water. As we stood in the upper dormitory, he seemed neither frail or in need of assistance. And when we descended the steep flight of stairs, I was thankful that he did not put me in the awkward position of wanting to help him without knowing how to do it discreetly and efficiently. He chatted even as we crossed the novitiate garden and, in the company of dozens of other visitors, neared the priory. There, his younger brother came rushing up to us, clearly in a panic, so much so that he even seemed to have forgotten the cigarillos. He immediately began scolding the older brother, pausing now and then to talk at me.

The ailing Belgian's healthy brother, I learned, was an Englishman and for years now, when the two of them were not in one of their apartments outside of Antwerp or in Brighton, they would be travelling—an aging couple without a marriage certificate, in which the younger was responsible for the constant care, while the older would make brief escapes like the one on which I had met him. As soon as the two were together again, his steps became unsteady and he stopped talking. His companion, in a friendly but decisive tone, suggested that we put off the Scotch that the older one had invited me to after five o'clock, by when the previously bright-eyed gentleman would have recouped with some rest. I vaguely agreed, even though I knew that by five I would have long since left Fontevraud and would be well on my way to Angers.

[...]

CHAPTER TWELVE

The Dolls of Arnstadt

I recommend you visit Arnstadt on an overcast summer day, in the morning, when the night storms are rolling away in the distance. The highway runs through damp green fields scattered with glowing poppies and the forests on the hillsides, almost black. The heavy grey clouds drift overhead. When they part, you catch glimpses of a cobalt-blue sky and, on the distant horizon, the forests regaining some colour. Then the wind shoves the banks of clouds together again and the landscape below, often praised for its beauty, takes on a dismal, cowering air.

The local chronicle proudly states that the town was mentioned in official documents dated as early as 704 CE and is one of Germany's oldest cities. Throughout the entire Middle Ages, thanks to its location on the Gera River and its tributary, the Wild Gera, its mills blossomed, craftwork and trade created an early middle class, and between 1703 and 1706 Johann Sebastian Bach worked here as the organist. The heart of the old city sits at an elevation, and if you walk along Turnvater-Jahn Straße on a Tuesday morning around ten o'clock, past the many branches of global stores, and take the narrow Badergasse to the market square, you'll find yourself facing a picture so captivating that you'll be tempted to disappear into it.

The spacious market square has an unusual, triangular layout: its short side consists of an arcade topped with galleries, while its two longer sides are lined with elegant, gabled townhouses. The true expanse of the square is not immediately apparent, as on Tuesdays it attracts crowds for the weekly market, though it would seem unimaginably modest to those drawn to Arnstadt during its centuries of prominence. On such market days in the Middle Ages and the early modern period, we are told, joiners, woodturners, potters, weavers and cobblers offered their wares, farmers of the nearby villages brought their sows, calves and cattle, geese, pheasants, partridges and quail found buyers, and even an excellent wine that was aged in this area of northeast Germany was traded by the bucketful.

The merchants of today, many of whom look like they toil endlessly in poverty, have nothing to offer but junk from the culture industry that sends only its cast-offs, cheap plastic toys and electronics, paraphernalia of crude home improvement, wall calendars from China that are already yellowed, rejected porcelain figures and all sorts of trinkets with peeling paint or women's underwear. It is inconceivable that eleven stands with loudspeakers blaring the same 'soulful' music from the identical assortment of cassettes can possibly sell enough to cover the expense and effort of setting up shop. It is also inconceivable that there is such a demand for lingerie suitable for a bodice-wearing age or that Arnstadters could run through the stacks of corsets.

Exhausted even before the morning is over, the merchants stand wearily behind their wares, but the many who finger this or that item, almost always put it back. The bags they carry are mostly full of groceries bought in the supermarket nearby. The shabbiness spread out before the elegant architectural backdrop is an eyesore and no matter

how I try to attribute some dignity to this marketplace as a counter-
point to the fortresses of consumption built on the outskirts of our
cities, I cannot convince myself.

This is not the paltriness one has learned to live with, and in
which one might find one's particular things, nor is it a reduction to
the essential that is customary in the region or even to what is flour-
ishing and produced in the region. What is offered, rather, is the
superfluous, not as luxury, however, but as remainders of some other
place, defective goods that are delivered in a damaged condition. On
such a day, it is chilly, but the Italian pastry shop, La Gondola, has
set tables outside from which you can watch the languorous goings-
on. Due to the unpleasant weather or the fact that people in the small
eastern German towns, which many residents are abandoning, don't
have much money, only one table is occupied: an old woman in
faded ochre clothing is sitting next to her granddaughter as the child
eats an ice-cream cone. The entire time, a bald man of about thirty
stands in the open doorway of the pastry shop, wearing a black
T-shirt that shows off his bizarrely deformed biceps and an upper
torso that none of the voluminous bodices could fit. As if he didn't
trust his own strength, he had a bull terrier sitting at his feet.

After you've drained your cup of coffee, you may find yourself
seized with the boyish ambition of testing your strength against the
man at the shiny cash register. So, I held my breath as I ambled past
him and his bull terrier and entered the pastry shop. He followed
me, threateningly close. I told him what I had consumed and in a
high falsetto he promptly named the modest sum I owed. He spoke
with an embarrassed smile as if asking a favour that made him
uncomfortable. In a squeaky soprano voice, he thanked me for the
coins I handed out, then accompanied me to the door past the

resting dog and its blood-thirsty eyes. When I turned back after a few metres, he gave me a timid wave.

From this end of the square, the life-sized monument at its centre catches your eye: a dark metal statue of a man leaning back, half-upright, half-perched on a kind of vague barstool—a self-confident young man who seems to be looking over mockingly at the passers-by. The figure has no trace of the solemnity that is present in all the portraits of Johann Sebastian Bach. Placed in this square by the sculptor Bernd Göbel in the GDR era, this statue of the 'young Bach' doesn't exactly depict him as a rebel, nor does it portray the pious composer renowned for his sacred music. Behind the statue is a Renaissance building, the House at the Palm Tree, with an exhibition that documents everything about Bach and Arnstadt —where he had composed his first fugues and toccatas and thirty-three organ chorales while engaging in endless disputes with the church authorities.

It began to rain when I set out from the House at the Palm Tree, walking uphill to the Church of Our Lady. The interior of this enormous building glows with hovering light and has earned it the designation of the most beautiful aisled hall church in Thuringia. I sat inside and contemplated the 'Beautiful Madonna of Arnstadt' who seems stern in her new motherhood until I was distracted by a man who was not-yet-old, accompanied by a woman who was no-longer-young, that is, he was about ten years older than I and she about fifteen years younger. From the way they stood next to each other, moved and spoke together, I couldn't tell if they were more likely father and daughter or a married couple or some other kind of couple and this uncertainty irritated me all the more because questions like these always disrupt my sense of calm no matter where I am. There

I was in the Church of Our Lady and instead of paying homage to the beautiful Madonna, all I could do was speculate whether the man's wife and his companion's mother had died and the two of them, having found a new attachment to each other in their grief, had set off on a trip together or if their situation was another one altogether.

If you leave the Church of Our Lady at midday, irritated at being disturbed by other visitors, Arnstadt will spread out before you in the sheen of a recently finished rain shower. This lends some buoyancy to your step, and you soon pass the market square where the first hawkers are stowing crates of unsellable goods in their cars and, via Zimmerstraße, you arrive at Schloßstraße. On this street, the Baroque Palace houses a museum in which you will find the model of the entire city from another era.

Princess Augusta Dorothea von Schwarzburg-Arnstadt lived for eighty-five years, many of which she spent as a pious widow, completely devoted to her pleasure. *Mon Plaisir* is what she called the doll town that she was forever expanding and that faithfully reflected life in a royal seat in the seventeenth century, including all social strata from the court to the travelling puppet show. The royal court is reproduced in miniature with its salons and bedchambers, state rooms and workshops, the bourgeois city with craftsmen's workshops and stores, houses and streets and the market with strolling people, travelling merchants and knife grinders. The doll town includes an entire pharmacy with delicate instruments, tubes, bowls, scales and vats, which takes up a full floor of the palace. Hundreds of figures—from the princess herself and her ladies-in-waiting to the nuns in the Ursuline Convent, from the Lord Chamberlin to the barber—are individually designed and added to the collection as representative of their social strata.

The widow lived a secluded life but was nonetheless connected to the world, her interest in which was determined primarily by what it could offer her *Plaisir*. Her intention for the doll town was to create with it an image of her city and her epoch. But wait, could she have foreseen that the time in which she lived would become an 'epoch' for future generations? More than an awareness of the transience of her own existence, did she also have what later came to be called historical consciousness? Even her ladies-in-waiting were required to contribute to the expansion of her doll town and industriously sew clothing for the countless small figures, stitch curtains for the interiors, and cover the sofas that measured a few centimetres in length with velvet. The survival of local faience makers depended on the princess, who had to borrow money from the aristocrats, yet continued to place orders with the craftsmen. The dolls' heads are made of beeswax combined with a secret mixture and it seems that in some of them, their nameless creators tried to capture with more than a touch of satire the greed, envy, boastfulness and stolidness of the models they took from daily life in Arnstadt. The doll town was meant to reproduce the social cosmos of all Arnstadt and this aspiration is what makes this work that was commissioned and supervised by the princess so unique. After all, the princess showed equal interest in every inhabitant of the social world of the dolls, no less in the beggar than in the highest-ranking chamberlain.

Travellers should not leave any town without visiting its cemetery. A municipal association maintains the old cemetery of Arnstadt in the impeccable state that seems to me, more than anything, to emphasize the mournfulness of these places all over the world.

Plaques indicate the way to the grave of Eugenie Marlitt—who ran a writing cottage industry in the nineteenth century, churning out monthly new episodes of novels that were kitschy and successful— and the grave of Willibald Alexis. Whereas Marlitt's novels, which grew ever-more romantic as her living circumstances deteriorated, were rediscovered by television (since Sunday afternoon programming cannot be filled with Rosamunde Pilcher alone), Alexis is not only interred under a beautiful granite block set up by his admirers more than 100 years ago, but also in the deep vault of literary history.

Late afternoon, evidently, is the time to leave Arnstadt, when the clearing clouds herald several days of beautiful summer. The endearing thing about dolls, I thought having left Arnstadt behind, is simply the flipside of their eeriness, and the quaint doll town is, in reality, a necropolis, a city of the dead through which the Princess Augusta Dorothea lives on after her earthly demise, and which reminds us as we walk through it that our own lives are passing.

Willibald Alexis: Apropos Arnstadt

There are two reasons that I, a literary omnivore who, as a young man, devoured the strangest rinds—some very hard to digest, indeed—found the Prussian journalist, novelist, travel writer and tireless newspaper publisher Willibald Alexis appealing. I don't believe that I'd have been drawn to much else in his writing, stamped as he was, on the whole, by that Prussian servile spirit, whose critic he fancied himself to be. But Alexis—who was born Georg Wilhelm Häring in Breslau and grew up in Berlin, pursued law; he was E. T. A. Hoffmann's colleague at the criminal court—won me over because he wrote about my native Salzburg. In his *Travels in Austria, Southern Germany and Switzerland*, he praised the beauty of Salzburg above all other places. But about the inhabitants, who had lived under the secular control of spiritual leaders and in 1833, at the time of Alexis' travels, had been subjects of the Habsburg Monarchy for less than twenty years, he wrote: 'The old saying, "life is good under the crozier", seems still fresh in their memories, but they associate with it entirely foreign commercial considerations.' Pious and commercial thoughts, religion as business which became a religion of business, business as the true religion of Salzburg, this is what this Prussian wanderer, who constantly held the Viennese as apt models for the Berliners, had incisively observed and formulated on his travels through Austria. (He did have one reservation, however: that Viennese did not know how to prepare beef.)

The other reason I had come up with earlier was that the idea of writing a 'Literary History of Failure', not a 'Tragic Literary History', like the one written by the Swiss Germanist Walter Muschg, who saw the tragic as an essential part of genius, but rather an imagined history of failed books, abandoned projects, the terrible consequences of success and washed-up talent. For such a literary history, the first book that Alexis published and that overshadowed his life as a writer would have been a prime example.

The Dan Brown of the early nineteenth century was a Scotsman named Walter Scott, whose books found countless readers (and imitators) throughout Europe. At the age of twenty-five, Willibald Alexis, grudgingly marking his hours in the bureau of investigations and dreaming of making his living by writing, published a massive historical novel, *Walladmor*. It was his greatest success and it offered him the chance to quit his position at the court and pursue writing.

On top of that, with this historical blockbuster set in Scotland in the Middle Ages, Alexis allowed himself a double joke. He published under the name of Walter Scott so that devoted German readers thought they had a novel by the famous Scottish novelist in their hands. And second, he offered a satirical critique of Scott's style.

At some point, Walter Scott got wind of a successful novel published in Germany under his name and decided, rather than bringing a suit against Alexis in a European court—which didn't even exist yet—to take much more cunning action. Scott had the German novel translated into English with only slight changes to the contents and presented it to his enthusiastic British readers as a new masterpiece. Alexis soon learned of this English appropriation of his book and, years later, on a trip through Scandinavia, he came upon a Swedish translation of *Walladmor* which, as far as he could tell, was based on his German version.

Alexis wrote many more historical novels under his own name and, with a logic that is not easy to follow, he again poached material from Scott's reservoir of Scottish myths. With each book, his literary style became ever-more subtle but ever-less popular. He kept his head above water by dashing off pieces of travel writing which he published first in newspapers then as anthologies. These volumes kept the Prussian censors on Alexis' heels although he had always hoped for liberally minded 'people's king', and never understood why the mere fact that he looked around in the world was enough to make him suspect. His newspaper ventures all went belly-up. He had to discontinue *Die Freimüthige* (The Outspoken), a daily paper he had founded and for which he alone produced all the content in 1835. His disappointment with the stifling of the 1848 Revolution freed Alexis from his political illusions and inspired his best work, not a masterwork but still a respectable piece that should be kept alive in literary history, not forgotten in its deep vault—his historical novel, *Ruhe ist die erste Bürgerpflicht* (Keeping Calm is the First Civic Duty, 1852).

At this point, he decided it was time to leave Berlin—where society was becoming militarized after the army had swept the protesting citizens from the streets—for idyllic Thuringia, preferably, Arnstadt. He soon bought a house, intending to fill the world with prolific articles and historical novels. However, not long after furnishing it, he suffered a stroke, and another followed a few years later.

He lived almost twenty more years in Arnstadt, far away from Berlin's literary circles, unable to speak or write. This most famous resident of the city was pushed in wheelchair by his wife everyday across the market square to the castle garden and back. A photograph from this time shows a man with features that must have once been prominent and angular with his head, covered with a sparse crown of hair, drooping over his chest. This was the man about whom the people of Arnstadt reverently murmured when they saw him passing in his wheelchair: 'In better days he wrote novels that were almost as important as Sir Walter Scott's incomparable *Walladmor*.'

Sir Walter Scott: A Footnote to Alexis

Walter Scott did not dare to publish his first novel under his own name. This aristocrat from one of the oldest and, admittedly, long impoverished and politically insignificant noble families of Scotland, published small editions of ballads and epic poems under his own name. But when writing *Waverley*, the first of many historical novels which gave birth to a new genre, he believed that publishing novels intended for a middle-class readership was beneath the dignity of an aristocrat. The success of *Waverley* was so massive that he wrote novel after novel in the same style. Until 1827, these novels appeared as 'By the Author of *Waverley*'. Only then did he brave the scandal of being a nobleman making money through the art of writing novels but by then the Author of *Waverley* was filthy rich and world famous.

Almost all of his novels are set between the twelfth and seventeenth centuries, a period he was so besotted with that, in 1812, he used his royalties to build himself a Gothic-style castle, Abbotsford House. Although he was the pioneer of the genre literary historians would later call the middle-class historical novel, the higher his print runs became to meet the demand of a growing middle-class readership, the more he retreated into a Medieval feudal dream world. He filled his fanciful estate with the threadbare vintage dross he had found in flea markets or old castles. He even received the countless admirers from all over Europe—who made their pilgrimage to Abbotsford House—dressed as a Scottish knight ready to set off for battle against the English, the Saracens or some other enemy of the ancient Gaelic land.

Surreptitiously, just as he had begun writing novels, he sought to increase his assets and became a silent partner of the publishing house that earned millions from his books. But his new business partner, the publisher, was no nobleman of the old Scottish type, but rather a middle-class entrepreneur whose reckless speculation led to his ruin. He ignobly disappeared to seek fortune elsewhere and left Scott, who had invested millions in his firm, in debt. Sir Walter considered repayment—for which he was blameless—to be a matter of honour which he had guaranteed with his noble name, and so he set to writing even more novels than before.

Every year, Scott produced hundreds of pages and, in fact, was able to repay almost every one of his creditors. After years of such prodigious overwork, he suffered an early stroke and, like his German middle-class disciple Willibald Alexis, who only fulfilled his life dream of a house in Arnstadt late in life, Sir Walter Scott spent his final years in his dream house in Abbotsford, paralysed and unable to read or write—a knight through and through, pushed in a small cart through his Romantic estate by nurses.

CHAPTER THIRTEEN

Europe–Africa: A Trip to Brussels

It is said that the sun sparkling through the ancient stained-glass windows of Notre-Dame des Victoires au Sablon is a God-given pleasure. However, one morning when I entered the church, I found myself in a gloom that the flickering candlelight barely penetrated. I thought I was alone until I noticed a man kneeling in the darkness in the pews under the organ loft. With his elbows propped on the railing and his face buried in his hands, he spoke silently to God. In a side aisle lay the grave of the unknown Rousseau—the ostracized poet Jean-Baptiste Rousseau, creator of strictly formal odes and venomous epigrams, one in a long series of refugees who had escaped to Brussels, where they were taken in and died as exiles. There was no sound in the church aside from a pious silence and the traffic rushing past in the rain outside on Rue de la Régence.

From the church's main door, I saw to the right the enormous Law Courts with its golden dome in the distance. The multi-lane Rue de la Régence, indicated on the sign as 'Regentschapsstraat', leads straight to it. Since the time of Mayor Buls, who led the city government around 1900, all the street signs in Brussels have been bilingual, unlike the city residents—I hardly met anyone who did not pretend to be unable to understand the other language. I walked along this boulevard for a few hundred metres and the closer I came to the Palace of Justice, cloaked in a drizzling mantle of rain, the uglier it seemed. The Palace of Justice, I realized, is more than just ugly, it is repellent: a colossal stone visage of power. The sheer scale of the palace, built in honour of injustice, is frightful, and the square before it, named after the architect whose vainglorious plans for the court's construction were drawn up in 1866, seemed to me equally enormous.

Joseph Poelaert had 3,000 buildings torn down to realize the commission given to him by King Leopold II and his mission to build the era's largest structure drove him mad. Four years before the completion of the Palace of Justice, a monument to the shared mega-lomania of architect Poelaert and his monarch, he died in a state of speechless mental derangement that no fame could assuage. His despotic patron, Leopold II, lived another twenty-five baleful years.

Born into the House of Saxe-Coburg and Gotha, Leopold devoted his life to becoming the sole owner of an African colony. First, he sent expeditions under the guise of philanthropy and scien-tific research to the upper reaches of the Congo River. Then, once it was certain that conquest and mass murder would be profitable, he ordered crushing military campaigns to conquer the land and enslave the population. The able-bodied were worked to death in mines and rubber plantations, and the guards—Belgian soldiers and Arab mer-cenaries—were ordered to shoot any African attempting to escape. Furthermore, because Leopold loved bureaucratic probity, they were commanded to chop off the hands of those who were shot and to deliver them to the colonial government in Leopoldville to prove the proper use of munitions.

Ten million Africans fell victim to his project. A poor country in the nineteenth century, all of Belgium's wealth stems from the reign of Leopold II. He plundered the Congo Free State for twenty years as a private entrepreneur using state bonds until he was ostracized by the great powers for his brutality, and he was forced to cede Congo to the Belgian state. When Leopold II's dead body was conveyed in the state carriage from the palace to the cemetery, the citizens of Brussels lined the road, whistling and booing wildly as the deceased made his way into national eternity.

The Palace of Justice is 160 metres long, 150 wide and 120 high. Its 26,000 square metres are divided into 245 rooms, including almost 30 courtrooms in which justice unceasingly tries the opponents of state and king. The largest structure built in Europe in the nineteenth century, it looms high over the city because it is located on the Rue de la Régence in the upper section of Brussels on hills that are considerably more elevated than the city's lower section with its older districts. Poelaert, I am sure, was already deranged when he began building and only recognized who he was when he went insane. The huge structure, bigger than Saint Peter's Basilica, is a stylistic muddle in which columns and pilasters a metre thick as well as Doric and Ionic columns dominate the heavy classicism that appeals to people of violent dispositions. The Palace of Justice is the end, not only for justice, but also for traffic because the street feeds into a roundabout next to a 30-metre drop off. Below the Palace lies the Marolles, the oldest neighbourhood of Brussels, reachable with a flight of stairs and, more recently, with an external glass lift.

I exited the lift under the benevolent gaze of Dr Joseph Kasa-Vubu, the first Congolese president. When in the Marolles, you are not only in Brussels but also another world which includes modern Africa and the old Flanders, welfare state managed poverty and commercially supported Bohème, urban decay that could still be checked and gentrification that has only affected certain streets and not yet permeated the entire neighbourhood. The larger-than-life, recoloured portrait of Kasa-Vubu was hung in the window of a small hut next to the lift, facing passers-by and festooned with all manner of African devotional objects. It seemed fittingly urban and historically accurate in an ironic way that 30-metre elevation separates the Palace of Justice built by Leopold II, the greatest criminal of all criminal colonial politicians, and a modest building bearing the name of the politician who signed Congo's declaration of independence. Unfortunately, Kasa-Vubu immediately accepted the eagerly offered assistance from the colonial powers when he sought to eliminate his opponent, the charismatic Prime Minister Patrice Lumumba, whom he later had murdered.

That was in 1960. Unlike the murdered Lumumba, Kasa-Vubu understood the liberation struggle as a tribal war over the privileges of the Bakongo, his own ethnic group. And yet this man, whose disastrous legacy haunts the land that suffered one tribal conflict after another, still has African and Belgian followers in Brussels. Joseph Kasa-Vubu studied Catholic theology, worked in the finance department of the Belgian colonial administration for more than a decade and after taking office as president, he decided to base his power on the military skills of a young officer known for his cruelty and greed. A few years later, this officer, who preferred to exploit the Congo's vast natural resources alone rather than share them with Kasa-Vubu's coterie, deposed the president, accusing him, no doubt accurately, of corruption.

The officer who led the coup changed his own name to Mobutu Sese Seko when he became the president. He was the African revenant of Leopold II, not only because he massacred millions in the Congo but also because he ran his country, which he renamed Zaire, as a vast private enterprise. At the end of his thirty-year rein, the personal wealth he had spirited away to Switzerland and other European countries was as great as the national debt while his countrymen went hungry because of the yearly interest owed to international banks. This African man identified so deeply with Leopold II that he erected a monumental equestrian statue of the Belgian king in the heart of the capital Kinshasa, formerly known as Léopoldville. When demonstrators demolished the statue, Mobutu saw it as a personal attack and used it as a pretext to monitor and harass the population even more extensively.

Hoogstraat is a narrow, a kilometre-long street that cuts almost straight through the French Marolles or the Flemish Marollen. The oldest street in Brussels, it runs almost exactly along the course it had in Roman times. The name Marollen echoes the Maricolles order of nuns who brought religious instruction and moral improvement to this neighbourhood of prostitutes and crooks in the seventeenth century. In his bleak reportage of Brussels after the Second World War, the Flemish writer Louis Paul Boon, one of greatest European social realists of the twentieth century who remains almost completely unrecognized in Europe, depicted the Marollen as a jungle of misery and disease. Today, Brusselers do not compare the Marollen to the Bronx as an area avoided by those concerned about personal safety, nor do they view it as a dangerous neighbourhood because it is underprivileged. Instead, they take pride in Marollen, seeing in it the spark of that ancient defiance, of the wit and urban culture of a marginalized people whom they consider the proto-Brusselers, their untamed ancestors.

These proto-Brusselers have developed their own dialect, although it is dying out in the country riven by endless conflicts over language. In this dialect the two warring languages, French and Flemish, were fused together and mixed with the old Spanish that the Sephardic Jews, who arrived like countless other refugees and immigrants brought to this country, no, to this city, and again no, to the Marollen. Brussels is a large city consisting of many villages and it is still said today that Brusselers could spend their entire lives in a village, without ever seeing the city of Brussels, that is, the grand, old metropolis of a kingdom, a colonial empire, a modern European state and the European Union. Even if the residents of the Marollen have not ventured into the city or the wider world, that world has come to them: the Marollen is the small world of the old multiculturalism that began to take shape in the early modern period, an era of exploratory voyages, long-distance trade, war and plagues—and hordes of refugees, travelling students, work emigrants moving here and there. The Marollen represents the colourful heritage of old Europe, which was so vibrant because it had not yet understood that it could be forced into uniforms of nation states. This worldly-wise culture from yesteryear now has to cope with the frantic immigration of outcasts from all continents and create a new multiculturalism.

Hoogstraat is lively at midday. Women in raincoats holding children's hands make their way to kindergartens or offices. Men stand together in groups, shivering and wet in their sweaters and jackets, and show that mornings can also be spent without activity. This was no African ghetto since square-built villagers with bulbous noses and florid faces passed these groups, rural Belgians, I would have guessed, had I not encountered in the centre of the city these figures who looked like they had emerged from the peasant tableaus of Pieter

Brueghel the Elder, who lived and died on Hoogstraat. Aside from the stubborn villagers who had been wandering unhurriedly through their neighbourhood for centuries, there were the fashionably dressed young people who seemed to be taking over every street and alley in the Marollen, people who could afford to live in more expensive areas of the city, but considered the raw, motley Marollen to be the most interesting part of Brussels.

When I turned the corner onto the gently rising Sistervatstraat, the Rue de la Rasière, I found myself in a brick housing development. This densely built social housing was constructed for the proletarians of 1900 and is now allocated to migrants from Africa, the Caribbean and the West Indies. There were more wastebins than cars, and although you could not miss the bins, signs were posted every few metres on walls and fences warning that littering was punishable by a €150 fine. The long-term residents of the Marollen and many of the recently arrived, I realized, were caught in daily street battle to keep their neighbourhood from turning into a slum.

This battle was already in progress at the large, square Place du Jeu de Balle, or Vossenplein, and the outcome seemed undecided. Soon after sunrise, the most famous flea market in Belgium sets up at this site. Twenty years ago, fine antique dealers did their daily rounds to stock up on favourably priced furniture that merely needed a touch of repair work for them to charge ten times the amount they paid here. But the present mood was gloomy. Most of the dealers stared morosely at the piles of their worthless, often defective merchandise and I recalled the improvised flea markets of Odessa that I had found so astonishing because warped and rusty wares they offered — broken lamps, single shoes, torn clothing . . . Ten years later, the peripheries of Europe had made their way into the capital of the European Union, yet instead of yesterday's affluence being peddled here, it was poverty's cast-offs. Ancient typewriters with missing keys and broken ribbon spools were tossed one on top of the other as if the vendors themselves were aware that they were selling nothing but garbage, electric appliances from the 1950s with important parts broken off, books and vinyl records strewn over the gravelly asphalt and in puddles . . .

The flea market seemed to have its social divides. On the one side, along the outer edge, better items were being sold by red-cheeked men who did not come from the countryside but had emerged from Brueghel's paintings of Flemish village life. The closer the stands were to the centre of the square and extending to the other side—from the Flemings to the Lebanese and Moroccans and on to the sub-Saharan Africans—the more picturesque the items which had not been arranged for display but simply dumped on the ground. No one in need is served by a broken record player or a refrigerator without a door. I looked around and saw that most of the people I had taken for vendors were acquaintances, friends or relatives of the vendors. Only occasionally did anyone pick up an object and turned over in their hands, then drop it carelessly on the clutter.

All the same, the Vossenplein was the only place in Belgium where the linguistic conflict had been resolved. Here, the Flemings did not have to pretend they did not understand French, and the Walloons did not have to pretend they could not understand Flemish. The languages that ruled this square were the African-French and the African-Flemish that sound like two dialects of a single, non-existent language, which, if it did come into existence one day, would be called Belgian.

On the southern side of the square is a church with a reddish-brown facade dedicated to the immaculate conception but informally called the Capuchin Church. It is the daily refuge for Marollen residents who sought brief respite from the stresses of living in this neighbourhood. When I entered the church, I found a group of African flea market vendors gathered for spiritual contemplation. They sat almost pressed together, as if helping each other reach a state of religious ecstasy. The sandwiches they had brought as a snack lay on the pew; they would eat them after praying as if to remember that it is a godly and good thing to refresh not only the soul but also the body in the house of the Lord.

Numerous signs offered information about all sorts of things: the Spanish-language mass that would be celebrated the following day; the local social services; announcing births and deaths; on Saint Anthony of Padua, whose pedestal was covered with notes that dozens of people had scribbled with thanks for their recovery. Yet the Capuchins kept silent about their most heroic deed. There was no mention anywhere that their church had been a place of refuge when the Wehrmacht occupied Belgium and special units of the SS were combing the Marollen. As soon as the Vossenplein was cordoned off, the monks opened their church to the threatened Jews and showed them a secret passage that ran 200 metres underground to the Rue des Tanneurs. Many Jews escaped their pursuers this way.

The Africans knew this story. They recounted it to me later with great excitement, interrupting each other, thrilled that someone wanted to hear it from the newcomers, which turned them into locals imparting information about their city. But they did not know who those people were who had to be rescued in this church or from whom they were escaping on the Rue des Tanneurs. They saw themselves both in those who were pursued and in those who helped them as good Christians.

Most of the shops on the Rue des Tanneurs had not yet opened by midday; their rolling shutters were down, as they may have been for months or years now. And yet, there were signs on this street that the residents were not prepared to give up. Many of the storefronts were empty but the display windows were not smashed, some apartments appeared uninhabited but the entrances were neat, and the facades had not yet been tagged by gangs. A noisy throng of schoolchildren passed in single file behind their teacher who shooed me off of the pavement with resolute cheerfulness while a few mothers in the rearguard kept watch to make sure no one strayed away. Maybe they were on their way to one of the many underpasses that connects the Marollen beneath the railway embankment to the north and beneath the Boulevard de Midi, the Zuidlaan, to the west with the neighbourhoods on the other side of the train tracks and the bypass.

I had stood in these underpasses an hour earlier; every inch was painted in loud colours by children. You could not tell which pictures were of Brussels and which of Africa, but the children had probably seen neither place: the African country their parents had left and Brussels, the large city surrounding their small village, which hardly anyone left even through a world-renowned old city centre was less than a fifteen-minute walk away. The railway embankment and the bypass road created a border and the border stones were bold children's paintings set neither in Brussels nor Africa, but in African Brussels, of which there is another, along with the Marollen, in a neighbourhood of Kinshasa called Matongé.

IN THE FOREST OF METROPOLES

At one point the dense rows of houses along the Rue des Tanneurs opened onto a vast development extending uphill. From my vantage below, I saw a wide panorama of municipal housing. I marvelled at the bustling expanse. The view was like a Brueghel painting you could step into. I saw the most peculiar figures busy with their daily routines: a woman in a brightly coloured, flowing robe carrying a heavy package on her head; a man with a black tunic and white trousers that billowed in the wind pulling a handcart, the likes of which I hadn't seen since I was a child, filled with a towering tangle of chairs; an old man of indomitable dignity with a long white beard, walking with a stick. I saw countless children playing age-old games with chalk squares on the pavement and teenagers on skateboards thundering down the long, steep roads that cut through the development. High above in the distance, I could see the bone-white cube—the Palace of Justice of the butchers who conquered Africa for themselves and for Belgium, and could not prevent conquest and plunder of Africa from spilling onto Europe, filling the entire neighbourhood at the foot of their palace with teeming life.

Speechless in Two Languages:
The Coiffeur Brahym and the Invention of Belgian

Monsieur Brahym rose with a start when I entered his small shop. The shabby two-storey building stood not far from the busy Boulevard du Midi in the centre of an empty space that was not a city square. Instead, the result from negligent city planning, it was, rather, an urban wasteland. I had been walking for a while in this peculiar area, almost in the heart of the city but abandoned by its residents and slated for demolition, until I happened on the building with 'Coiffeur Brahym' written in large letters on its water-stained facade.

At that moment, I recalled my aversion when I looked in the mirror on getting out of bed and saw a man who was ten years older than I, his shaggy grey hair standing on end, and I entered the barbershop.

Monsieur Brahym sat with two men around a low table. Like him, each had a slender, green ornamented glass of tea. Like them, Monsieur Brahym wore black trousers, a white shirt and a dark brown jacket. Perhaps he looked so startled because I was his only customer that day—on which not one of the three would have bet— or perhaps because he was aware of the impression of idleness he would make on me, a brash intruder stepping into his little piece of the Maghreb, as he sat there, busy with his friends and the passage of time. Monsieur Brahym wore a white, crocheted cap as a head covering, which struck me as an unsuitable item of a coiffeur's work clothes; also, his companions' short-cropped hair did not give me much confidence in the art of the master who considered my mop of hair at length and then shook his head regretfully, as if it would present him with far too difficult problems. So instead of a haircut, I received a glass of recklessly sweetened tea.

My conversation with Monsieur Brahym and his two friends was stimulating, even if I could not say what language we conversed in. Some of what I heard reminded me of the tongue I had first taken for French, its diphthongs stretched by some speakers as if they wanted it to sound like Dutch. Like two days prior at the flea market in Vossenplein—it seemed to me that precisely among recent immigrants, I was hearing the country's missing language: Belgian. Still, in Maghrebi Brussels you can try speaking in French or in Dutch and your conversational partner will notice efforts made to understand and be understood unlike the long-established residents of Brussels, who, when mistakenly addressed in the wrong one of the city's two languages, will not go to any trouble to try and understand you and furthermore will take malicious satisfaction in not being understood by you.

That morning, I had gone to the international literature house Passa Porta to ask the director what I should take into consideration for my reading in keeping with the spirit and conventions of the city. She showed me everything, the small green room to which a short flight of stairs led from the lecture hall, where the writers could meet with their moderator or translator before the reading over small sandwiches and beverages, the well-stocked bookstore, the gallery with photographs of the writers who already had their memorable— for good or ill—readings behind them. She was a pleasant woman, a few years younger than I, plump, with almost colourless hair and warm, twinkling eyes. I had spoken to her in French and at first I didn't even notice that she was answering me in Dutch and, when I couldn't follow her, she switched easily to English. No Walloon living in Brussels would ever speak Flemish and no Fleming would speak French unless required by an administrative position or profession. 'You crunch and hiss in two languages,' the Flemish poet Willem M. Roggemann wrote about Brussels and the Flemish and Walloon residents of the city whose mother tongue is Dutch or French and who would rather speak to foreigners in English than in the national language that is not their own.

Most Walloons don't understand their cities' and country's other languages. In Brussels, where they are in the majority compared to the Flemings, all street signs are in two languages, but if you ask a Walloon for directions using the Flemish name, they are unable to help because they really don't know that the unpronounceable Huidevettersstraat is their Rue des Tanneurs. The Flemings, in turn, know what the French translation of the Dutch name sounds like, but they would rather not. As a result, they can only claim ignorance to foreigners since the Belgian state requires them to use the despised French language for many civic matters. Like the Germans and the Czechs in Prague in 1900, the Walloons and Flemings in Brussels have lived beside each other for years and, as in Prague—and all the more in Trieste—very few of the writers have crossed the invisible language barrier by translating the works of their Flemish colleagues into French or of their Walloon colleagues into Dutch.

The linguistic autism of the two leading nations in this multi-national state, which generously supports its small German minority in Eupen-Malmedy, is peculiar. The Flemish Simon Stevin, an important mathematician in the Renaissance who published ground-breaking works on hydrostatics, sought to prove in all seriousness through his passionate study of linguistics that the language spoken by Adam and Eve was Flemish and that all other languages in the world have derived from this primordial language. The Jacobins in turn, when they seized power over France, decreed that French was the language of freedom, democracy and human rights, but did not count the right to one's own mother tongue as a human right.

For the entire nineteenth century, even when Belgium had become an independent state, the Walloon elite used language policies to suppress Flemish as a rustic dialect and scorned it as the language of the clergy from whose influence the rural fools needed to be saved. After the Second World War, the Flemings were collectively suspected of having collaborated with the German occupiers and consequently, hundreds of thousands of them gradually switched languages, especially those aligned with the workers movement. But Wallonia, whose industry contributed to the economic and cultural dominance of French-speaking Belgium, has long been one of Europe's crisis zones. Now, it's Flanders that is one of the wealthiest, most economically successful regions of Europe. And the regionalism that in many areas of Europe seeks to break up the old structure of the state with its cohesion of richer and poorer parts of nations and draws on social egoism to foment the revolt of the affluent has created a powerful political movement in Flanders in which outrage over past injustices and arrogance form and explosive combination.

No bi-lingual street or town signs will help. In Belgium these are not indications of tolerance but of benign indifference. They are an acknowledgment that in the country everything must be done twice because two different peoples live in their own two worlds in the same city. In Brussels as a result, either the Flemish or the Wallonian fire trucks respond to a call depending on who reported the blaze, and while a Flemish ambulance rushes to pick up the man suffering a heart attack on Huidevettersstraat, a Wallonian ambulance is dispatched when the man collapses in the very same place on the Rue des Tanneurs.

So they squabble, no, not squabble, rather, they have taken up a comfortable stance of mutual ignorance and neither side wants to antagonize the other. 'Il n'y a pas de Belges,' there are no Belgians— this reason of state is the foundation of the Belgian nation which the Walloons and the Flemings have carved up into the most absurd bureaucratic construct. Brussels' tolerance is renowned; people from more than 100 countries live without fear of harassment in this city, the capital of the European Union, but hardly that of the Flemings and Walloons. The Flemings and Walloons, one can assume, are so fond of newcomers and foreigners because they cannot stand each other and don't want to be left alone with each other in their beautiful city.

It was not Monsieur Brahym who explained this to me. Rather, he explained the right way to brew tea and exactly when to add the sugar. He spoke with a guttural emphasis on the consonants and mixed the two national languages with a few others. There are no Belgians, you say? There are, indeed.

Louis Paul Boon: A Rereading

More than twenty years ago, I happened on Louis Paul Boon's books, then I searched for them methodically. What was it that I liked about him? Probably that he wrote about the downtrodden but refused to make any concessions to their literary taste. And that he seemed to me to be a true socialist who nonetheless did not believe in the promise of a classless society. He preferred day labourers, maids, the soot-blackened workers of the industrial districts, the despairing yokels who never made it out of their villages in Flanders, but he was neither a Romantic of the revolution nor a functionary of the class struggle. Wherever the oppressed dared to rise up, he was on their side, though he did not expect many results, certainly not his own deliverance, the deliverance of the intellectual who longed for more than sitting alone at his desk: to serve progress, to serve freedom or some other cause.

Before my trip to Brussels, I had taken his books from the shelf, less concerned that they might not be good travel reading than that their fervent tone might now, in a different time, possibly sound hollow to me. In that case, I'd only be able to read Boon in a doubly historic sense because I would relate the vanished world that was his to the other vanished world that was mine as a reader twenty years ago.

In his reportage on the jungle of Brussels, Boon tells the story of a Flemish maidservant who moves to the capital from the countryside. Even in old age, she knows very little about this city, apart from the Rue Haute, where the hospital is, and the Rue Blaes, where there is a shop for servants. Blaesstraat runs parallel to Hoogstraat, cutting through the Marollen from the upper city to the centre. The way Louis Paul Boon describes his nameless heroine, you sense that he is devoted to her and can respect and love her without feeling the need to idealize her. He doesn't endow her with any attributes that would make her a class-conscious rebel or a precursor of the new human beings, the idea of which intoxicated so many revolutionaries for whom the old human beings with their weaknesses and flaws were not enough.

Boon casually dismissed the fame that caught up with him in his old age as 'Boonapartism'. He had been attacked for too long on political or religious, national or aesthetic grounds for him to be assuaged with the title of national writer. In 1972, seven years before his death, he narrowly missed winning the Nobel Prize which was awarded to Heinrich Böll—but what does that matter? For decades, he was a target for the scorn of a wide variety of minds. Not all of them expressed themselves as drastically as the Belgian critic who, in 1943, when the National Socialists had already invaded the country and deviation from literary norms could be dangerous, declared in a screed about his early novels: 'The race of writers to which Boon belongs should be exterminated. They poison everything they touch ... Such novels make me long for the time when a great pyre will be built here too.'

Nazi collaborators were not the only ones who had something against this Flemish Balzac. Catholics considered him a pornographer; the conservatives suspected him—not without good reason— of being a political insurgent; those in sophisticated literary circles turned up their noses at this coarse, small-town fellow because of the forcefulness of his complaints and accusations; and the communists, whose resistance efforts he had joined against the occupiers of Belgium, soon criticized his socially critical prose for not offering the prospect of a better world and the classless society of tomorrow.

Indeed, in many of his novels and stories, Boon follows traces of social revolutions and political uprisings, but almost every one of these chronicles of humiliation and outrage, violence and resistance ends in defeat. He firmly believed that it was necessary to rise up against injustice, but at the same time he was convinced that either the wrong ones would win in any case or, if the right ones did prevail, that their proud flight would quickly fall to earth again and harden into a new power.

The appeal of his narratives is connected with such contradictions, which the author does not try to cover up. Instead, in each new book he explores them afresh, even heightens them. Boon lent his voice to the outcast, the disadvantaged, to those who had ended up in the gutter, and yet he was a pessimist who did not believe in a better future for them or a more humane future for all. Anyone who is as convinced of the necessity of the struggle as of the inevitability of its failure will find his integrity to be at risk. Louis Paul Boon knew that he had to protect himself from a destiny that I would call Austrian, that is, the fate of unintentionally—although perhaps unwitting contributing to—becoming an author beloved of those who conveniently opt for cynicism and a misanthropy well-justified by the humanity's wickedness: 'The most difficult struggle in life is to resist becoming embittered.'

One of his masterpieces, *Chapel Road*, a two-volume novel about an industrial city in Flanders and a proletarian family, expresses the author's credo in the opening sentences. Boon writes that on the one hand, through his protagonist's difficult life which began around 1890 he wanted to draw a sketch of nothing less than 'the laborious RISE OF SOCIALISM, and of the decline of the bourgeoisie which got knocked down by two world wars and collapsed'. On the other hand, through the arc drawn from the misery of the turn of the century to the middle of the next and from the dirt-ridden mass housing for workers to the union officials' offices, Boon also wanted to show the imminent end of this movement whose laborious rise he had sketched so sympathetically. This novel of the rise of socialism contains the desperate 'search for something that could still check the DECLINE OF SOCIALISM' and 'for values that really count'.

Louis Paul Boon was born in 1912 in the poor district of Aalst, a small provincial city stricken by all the great wars of the centuries. He was destined to be an automobile varnisher or house painter until he—half-revolutionary, half-bohemian—followed his artistic talent down several wrong paths and blossomed first as a painter, then as a writer. He remained bound to the Aalst region between Ghent and Brussels, and drew on its various historical eras in his novels.

The bandit novel, *Jan de Lichte and his Band*, turns back to the middle of the eighteenth century: 'We lived in a time of famine, of plague and cholera and of many foreign soldiers. The Spanish were only just here and murdered our cities, and most of our people fled in haste across the Moerdijk. Then the Austrians came. And now, at the moment our book begins, the soldiers of the French King Louis XV have invaded our country.'

In *Jan de Lichte*, Boon tells an exciting story that was almost forgotten in Aalst where it once took place. It is the sordid yet uplifting story of a bunch of vagrants who, led by Jan de Lichte, become a gang of robbers and soon control the entire province. The band is then crushed, and de Lichte is betrayed and broken on the wheel on the Aalst market square in 1748. He is but one of many bandits in a Europe shaken with upheaval. A few of these bandits became renowned as folk heroes and their fame lives on in songs and legends like those of the Magician Jackl from the Lungau region of Salzburg, Matthias Klostermayr of the Bavarian forests, Johannes Karasek of Lusatia, the Transylvanian Pintea the Brave or the much-lauded Ondraszek of the Silesian Beskid Mountains, made immortal by the Czech poet Óndra Łysohorsky.

Jan de Lichte evolved from a hot-tempered outlaw to a noble Robin Hood but then regressed again to a cruel robber chief, driven to fear his greedy followers and especially the legends that preceded him wherever he went, which he had to bolstered with ever new heroic deeds: 'It's not Jan de Lichte who formed a gang, instead the times have become ripe with 30,000 beggars in Brabant, 60,000 beggars in Flanders . . . The drumrolls sound and he, Jan de Lichte, is unable to divert the course of history in the slightest.'

This is Louis Paul Boon's point: man becomes the subject of his own fate and does not simply remain its object. But it rare for leaders or subordinates to alter even slightly the course of history, which is their own history, after all. Boon does not overload his historical figures with problems that are a worry for him, the later-born author, rather than for him. Still, in his folk hero novel, Boon manages to address, as if in passing, essential questions about revolutionary movements: Jan de Lichte's rebellion is a righteous one as long as his anarchic drive, the momentum of spontaneously taking matters into his own hands, remains effective. But to reach the just social order he dreams of, de Lichte has to lead the struggle and with this estrangement from the struggle, the old vices creep in and selfishness and cruelty, greed and vengefulness spread through the gang. In this novel, Boon portrays the rebellion of poor people who are plagued by misery. He views them with sympathy but does not over-estimate them. He has no illusions about the grounds or limits of their rebellion.

Also in his slender book, *My Little War*, Boon tells the stories of little people who are not better people simply because their lives are harder. Published in 1946, it divides the Second World War into snapshots, individual images, segments of narrative and fragmentary stories. This unusual form with its breakneck pace that recalls a film with hard, rapid cuts brings to life the Great War's devastating effects on the small and on provincial daily life, on the lives of the fearful and the courageous, of the selfish and the magnanimous.

Curiously enough, by splintering the war into apparently unre-lated fragments and disconnected details, Boon makes it recogniz-able. These are flashes of light that illuminate the night of war and fall gleaming on the betrayal and brutalization of man. The narrator punctuates the episodes and fragments that make up his Brueghelian picture of the Flemish people suffering adversity and temptation with comments that insert him into the storyline: 'For one would write words born of sweat and mire and dying horses attached to a wagon with its wheels in the air and through the atmospheric pres-sure created by devastated city blocks and blood. With such words one would form sentences like stricken tracks that begin quite nor-mally but after a short distance twist up into the air—as if the bombed trains had wanted to reach heaven—then after a stretch, the tracks crash to the ground again.'

Louis Paul Boon considered one of his best novels a failure. *Abel Gholarts* plays with some elements of Vincent van Gogh's life in a wonderfully lyrical way, but engages even more with his imagery, which Boon manages to capture in all its density because he himself had learned how to see landscapes as a painter. *Abel Gholarts* is not a fictional biography or even a *roman à clef*. Rather, it is a tableau of Flanders in the last third of the nineteenth century, a heart-wrenching book about life and death in the desolate provinces where all life dreams are crushed and even small joys are beyond reach.

Against the backdrop of a landscape drenched in gloomy rain and blazing sun, Boon tells the story of a sensitive child whose sense of hidden gifts are a torment rather than an inspiration. Laden with a sense of guilt, this child is always on the brink of breaking down. The book ends with Abel Gholarts starting to paint a canvas that is unmistakably van Gogh's early masterpiece, *The Potato Eaters*. Louis Paul Boon respected potato eaters. Maybe that is why he, one of the greatest social realists of the twentieth-century European literature, counts for so little in era when some are stuffed with French fries and others shave slices off truffles.

Charles-Joseph de Ligne in Beloeil and the Kahlenberg: One More Step to the Side

I was asked if I wanted to visit Beloeil, which is located not too far from Brussels, near the French border and easily reached by car. On the one hand, strictly designed gardens in which nature is pruned in the Baroque style and furnished with marble statues, stone nymphs and small temples have always made me sad. On the other, the Beloeil Castle grounds are considered the most elegant park in Wallonia. That said, I had long harboured feelings of sympathy for the creator of Beloeil, whom Goethe called the merriest man of the century, and I did not want to spoil my affection by visiting his garden, a celebrated masterwork of nature made art, and exposing myself to that vague sadness which, since my childhood, has inevitably washed over me every time I entered an ornamental garden.

He himself, the Seventh Prince de Ligne, believed that sadness was an outrage against the beauty of life and an unforgivable state and that every person of spirit and character was duty-bound to avoid it even under the most adverse conditions. Every one of his contemporaries who mentioned him in their letters or writings, singled out his constant friendliness, conviviality, his esprit and the thoughtfulness which he employed to join everyone, even feuding parties, in spirited conversation as character traits that first struck them and which the prince maintained to the end in the face all difficulties. He had mastered the art of not granting unhappiness any power and of resisting the lures of melancholy, and he, who left posterity thirty-four sizable volumes of his writings, once wrote that not a single novel was to be found among them because the death of one of his characters would have made him too sad.

This reverence for life is surprising in a man who was trained in the art of warfare, who, as a young man, had passionately pursued fame on the battlefield and who, in old age, published many books with descriptions of battles and studies of strategy. At the time, war took its toll primarily among those who were not seeking the glory of honourably bleeding to death in a morass but had been conscripted against their wills. In contrast, for the officers from the high aristocracy, of which Charles-Joseph de Ligne was one of the most renowned in all of Europe even at the age of twenty-five, the perpetual wars were to be considered one of the arts: and even then artists had no fatherland. Charles de or Karl von Ligne could count four countries as his 'fatherland' and at various times he held political or military positions in each of them, even though these fatherlands were often at war with each other: Russia, Austria, France and Belgium. In Belgium, which was never completely confident of its national cohesion, the Prince de Ligne was one of very few who, into the twentieth century, were hailed as heroes by both the Flemings and the Walloons. He was born in 1735 in Belgium, in the county of Hainaut, and there he built his arcadia Beloeil. For him, France's cultural supremacy was self-evident and Nietzsche claimed that the most elegant French prose stylist of the eighteenth century was not a Frenchman but the Belgian Charles de Ligne. He served in the Austrian imperial army as a young man and after the French revolutionists first courted him then later appropriated his immense wealth—which included Beloeil and its grounds, the castle and the 25,000-volume library—he settled permanently in Vienna at the age of sixty.

There he lived in a house on the Kahlenberg, married to a princess of Liechtenstein, saw several of their seven children die and, undaunted in his devotion to happiness and man's true purpose, continued to write his life's work, the thirty-four volumes of *Mélanges militaires, littéraires et sentimentaires*, a loosely organized chronicle of his inner and outer lives that touched on almost all the major topics of the day.

Three months before I travelled to Brussels and politely declined the offer of a ride to Beloeil, I had stood at the Prince de Ligne's grave, which lies well-concealed in a cemetery in a small forest on the Kahlenberg. It was a beautiful late summer day. We had driven up the Kahlenberg from Josefdorf and continued climbing another

200–300 metres along a narrow, curving road to a few steps leading into a cemetery that took pains to be inconspicuous and remain undetected. The first grave, uphill a few steps to the left of the half-open iron entrance gate, holds the remains of Karoline Traunwieser, whom the Orientalist Joseph von Hammer-Purgstall, one of the most peculiar figures in Austrian intellectual history, had called the 'most beautiful of the beauties'. Her reputation as the most enchanting of young women dancing at the balls of the Congress of Vienna lived on in legend and song for two generations after she died at the age of twenty-one. Near her grave is the monument of Charles-Joseph de Ligne, his wife and their granddaughter, Countess Sidonie Potocki, a stone rectangle, roughly 8-metre-long and 3-metre-wide. Two intensely green shrubs and a tree grow between the graves. In the tree's branches, birds sang joyfully, as they always have, and the hum of the city rose from far below.

There are now fewer than ten graves in this cemetery. The bones of the Polish Resurrectionist monks who tend the cemetery are buried in a communal grave. Some teenagers seemed to have chosen this place that appeared to have fallen out of time as their gathering spot. Empty bottles of Eristoff vodka were neatly lined up in two circles around a tree and on an old white gravestone that no longer recalled any particular person buried there 150 or 200 years ago since time had washed away the name. Instead, the teens had written a memento of their friends in black spray paint: 'Alex and Sabrina. 1987–2006.'

As a child, I had learned how to do quick mental arithmetic when visiting cemeteries with my parents. Today still, out of habit, the first thing I do at each grave is calculate how many years the person buried there lived and compare that number to my current age.

Sabrina and Alex, happy or unhappy in love, only made it to nineteen. I had already outlived them by thirty-five years. And Charles de Ligne was seventy-nine when the joy of living he had demanded everyone honour was taken from him, and he was buried in the cemetery on the Kahlenberg in December 1814.

He called many of his works fragments, others *écarts*—asides or sidesteps. He wrote quickly and gracefully, but without ambition. He considered literature a charming pastime, a tool to help people do to themselves what he had done to nature in the gardens of Beloeil. '*Corrigez la Nature*', was his mission, to alter nature in such a way that it becomes an expression of style and taste, in other words, so that it becomes culture. Correcting his own human nature, creating a version of his life in which he could lead it as a work of art and be admired, that was his ideal and literature was a means to achieve this self-education. That said, it was not only a means to this end; it was also an experience of happiness. *Écarts*, with all its ambiguity, suits the literary form very well for this is an author who is tempted by each idea that comes to him, delights in it, marvels at himself in thought and is constantly leaping from one idea to another. He digresses, then returns to his subject only to abandon it anew. He switches times, places, characters. Now he creates portraits of great men he has met, from the Emperor Josef II to Frederick the Great—whose meeting in Neisse in 1870 he in a sense moderated—from Voltaire to Madame de Staël, from Goethe to Wieland, from Rousseau to Casanova.

He offered the politically persecuted Rousseau refuge in Beloeil—what an image: the critic of civilization, who preached a return-to-nature, in a place where nature's wild growth was tamed to a finely chiselled showpiece of the Rococo! Indeed, Rousseau preferred to spend his exile elsewhere, restlessly changing cities. Casanova met de Ligne after he had escaped his captors in Venice and fled to Count Waldstein's Dux Castle in Bohemia, where he spent his final fourteen years as a librarian. De Ligne penned a marvellous portrait of Casanova, who had to play the fool for the nobility, once he was no longer the mocking wit, the renowned adventurer and envied lover, but an aging man, pursued by creditors. The proud, often humiliated Casanova, who 'would be a handsome man, if he were not ugly,' de Ligne tells us, has many talents, 'The only things he does not know are subjects in which he claims to be well-versed: the rules of dance and of the French language, the laws of good taste, of the way of the world and of *savoir vivre*. It is only his comedies that are not comical. Only his philosophical works that lack philosophy; the rest are filled with it; they always have some wisdom, something new, piquant, profound.'

Creating a fictional character instead of describing an historical figure is only a small literary sidestep. A gallery of oddball characters could be extracted from de Ligne's chronicles. Incisive, witty portraits are scattered throughout his writings, small building blocks for a major characterology like the one presented by Jean de la Bruyère 100 years earlier in *Caractères*. Unlike de la Bruyère, whose character studies Elias Canetti relished, Charles de Ligne does not remain bound by the conventions of his time in the characterization of women. Speculating about the nature of woman was foreign to him. He considered women to be characterologically far more complex and interesting than men, all of whom he found almost indecently alike in mind and heart.

The prince can certainly not be reproached for going into exile and leaving his wealth and estates behind without regret or for not paying attention to social issues during the last years of his life, which he spent in modest circumstances. When he wrote of people whose *art de vivre* he wanted to foster, he meant aristocrats by birth or those citizens who, through talent and hard work, became aristocrats of the mind. What he extolled was the daily discipline of persons of rank or intellectual elevation who had trained themselves to be cheerful. He was ready to forgive them any misstep, deviation or faux pas, except for despair. The Prince de Ligne described the childhood training he suffered at the hands of an unimaginative father who was constrained by prejudices of his class. With effort, he drove out the 'fear of having a bit more pleasure' that had been inculcated in him.

Thirty years ago, I was fortunate to find a selection of his writings in a crate at a flea market that seemed to specialize in yellowed, mildewed and damaged books. The selection, published in 1960, was edited by a man who was already as old as the hills, an Austrian exile who had fled the National Socialists to Sweden and did not feel at home in Austria after 1945—the son of the famous newspaper publisher Moritz Benedikt. In the shaky handwriting of an elderly man suffering from Parkinson's, Ernst Benedikt had dedicated the book to an aristocratic lady whose heirs cleared out her library a few years later. As a result, for a meagre sum, I became the owner of the book that sent me on the traces of the Prince Charles-Joseph de Ligne. Benedikt had given the book a title that no one would dare use for their own autobiography: *Genius of Life*. But that, exactly, is the heart of the matter.

POSTSCRIPT

It took many real and imagined journeys for me to come up with the idea of writing this book: journeys around my own room and across half of Europe, journeys through books and landscapes. Even my own life journey played a part. My twelve-year-old self in the mid-sixties, to name just one example, heard of Vuk Karadžić at the kitchen table from my father who was a great storyteller. I can no longer pinpoint exactly who first set me on which trail I followed on my own nor to which novels, studies and translations I owe which inspirations. But this is certain: I have quoted from Ivan Cankar's works in the eight-volume edition translated and annotated by Erwin Köstler for the Drava Verlag. Tudor Arghezi's poem is from the volume *Ketzerberichte*, translated by Heinz Kahlau, published in the GDR in 1968 by the publisher Volk und Welt. Margul-Sperber's poems were selected and beautifully annotated by Peter Motzan in the collection *Ins Leere gesprochen* (Rimbaud Verlag, 2002). And it was the wood engraver and publisher Christian Thanhäuser who brought the Bohemian-Portuguese František Listopad to my attention with the 2008 Thanhäuser edition of *Jahrmarkt Böhmen*, vividly translated by Eduard Schreiber.

I would like to thank all those who helped in word or deed in their cities and countries: Karin Cervenka (Bucharest), Teresa Kudyba (Opole), Lászlo Végel and Zlatko Krasni in Serbia, Pier

Carlo Bontempelli (Naples), Klaus Zeyringer (Angers), Wolfgang Günter (Patmos). And the friends who accompanied me on various stretches: Ria and Robert, Katharina and Thomas, Brigitte and Kurt, Fanny and Klemens, Milena and Benjamin. They can all vouch that everything was completely different.

TRANSLATOR'S NOTE

Where adequate English translations of texts in languages other than French or German quoted by Karl-Markus Gauß do not exist, I translated the quotes into English from the German translations he cites in his essays. The exceptions are lines from Tudor Arghezi's 'Song on a Flute' come from *Selected Poems of Tudor Arghezi*, translated by Michael Impey and Brian Swann (Princeton University Press, 2016) and those from Louis Paul Boon's novel are quoted from *Chapel Road*, translated by Adrienne Dixon (Twayne Publishers, 1972).

In this edition, Chapter Eleven appears in a slightly abridged form.

I would like to thank the National Endowment of the Arts and the Österreichisches Gesellschaft für Literatur in Vienna for their support of this translation. I am deeply indebted to Karl-Markus Gauß for his trust, patience and encouragement as I journeyed through his forest of metropoles.